C000265339

Emotional Coaching

A practical programme to support young people

A Lucky Duck Book

Emotional Coaching

A practical programme to
support young people

Robyn Hromek

P·C·P
Paul Chapman
Publishing

© Robyn Hromek 2007

First published 2007

Apart from any fair dealing for the purposes of research or private study, or criticism or review, as permitted under the Copyright, Designs and Patents Act 1988, this publication may be reproduced, stored or transmitted in any form, or by any means, only with the prior permission in writing of the publishers, or in the case of reprographic reproduction, in accordance with the terms of licences issued by the Copyright Licensing Agency. Enquiries concerning reproduction outside those terms should be sent to the publishers.

Rights to copy pages marked as handouts, certificates or overhead foils are extended to the purchaser of the publication for his/her use.

The right of the author to be identified as Author of this work has been asserted by him/her in accordance with the Copyright, Design and Patents Act 1988.

 Paul Chapman Publishing
A SAGE Publications Company
1 Oliver's Yard
55 City Road
London EC1Y 1SP

SAGE Publications Inc.
2455 Teller Road
Thousand Oaks, California 91320

SAGE Publications India Pvt Ltd.
B-42, Panchsheel Enclave
Post Box 4109
New Delhi 110 017

Commissioning Editor: George Robinson
Editorial Team: Mel Maines, Sarah Lynch, Wendy Ogden
Designer: Nick Shearn

A catalogue record for this book is available from the British Library

Library of Congress Control Number 2006904081

ISBN13 978-1-4129-2015-5
ISBN13 978-1-4129-2016-2 (pbk)

Printed on paper from sustainable resources

Printed in Great Britain by The Cromwell Press Ltd, Trowbridge, Wiltshire

Contents

Introduction

Resilient kids 'bounce back' from the inevitable crises that come along. Most young people are skilled in dealing with frustration, teasing, disappointments and generally maintain good relationships. For others, emotional control is tricky and any perceived threat is met with furious, sometimes physical defence or taken to heart and added to a store of negative self-concept. Inherited characteristics and the nurturing experience set up patterns of responses, physiology kicks in and emotional first-aid is needed. These young people need a supportive team of people who understand the nature of emotional difficulties and are willing to maintain relationships with them. This team will include parents, teachers, coaches, and when necessary, psychologists and child psychiatrists. With education, skill development and social support, most young people with mild to moderate emotional difficulties will develop adaptive coping skills.

Coaching provides a chance to invent new and promising futures with young people through goal setting and skill development. Emotional coaching focuses on deciphering and managing emotions in one's self and others. Coaches are able to mediate between young people and emotional crises in a way that empowers them to take responsibility for their reactions and increase self-regulation. There are risks as well, for both coaches and students, depending on the quality and duration of the relationship. Research suggests the longer and the more supported the coaching programme is, the better. This means people from the 'natural' settings of extended families, communities and schools – teachers, counsellors, psychologists, heads, deputies, aides – make excellent coaches. As part of the immediate environment they are able to debrief young people and provide support. Volunteers who are not from the child's immediate social and educational worlds must be prepared to commit to coaching for long periods of time. Coaches without a background in education or psychology will require training and ongoing support structures for the experience to be effective.

The thoughts and ideas in this book are based on research and years of experience as an emotional coach to children and young people. They are based on the belief that young people are a work in progress and for most, emotional and behavioural problems are just a phase. Most children have the capacity to change and are not 'locked in' by early experiences; however, early intervention is a must when difficulties are identified. Programmes that include cognitive behavioural therapy (CBT), guided imagery, relaxation, slow breathing and behavioural changes etc. are effective in teaching children about emotional regulation. The 'tricks' and 'spells' referred to in this book are helpful things to do and say to assist with self-calming. Young people with mild to moderate difficulties will benefit most from this kind of coaching. Serious difficulties should be assessed and treated by a child psychiatrist with a team working to support the young person, her family and the school. Sometimes medical interventions are needed before young people are in a 'frame of mind' to use CBT and relaxation strategies.

The emotional issues addressed in this book are common themes amongst the challenges faced by young people: friendships, teasing, anxiety, anger, depression, schoolwork and happiness. The chapters set out current understandings around the issues, who should benefit, what to cover in coaching sessions and when to refer on to other professionals. The reflection sheets and games reinforce teaching around each theme and are designed for use with individuals, small groups and in the classroom to teach about emotions.

Finally: many blessings on the people who count it a privilege to work with children and young people at risk of disadvantage within our societies.

How to use the CD-ROM

All the printable items for the games are on the CD-ROM in PDF format. You will need Acrobat version 4 or higher to view and print these files.

There are seven named folders on the CD-ROM, containing the gameboards, game cards, reflection sheets and other items needed for each game.

Gameboards - Gameboards are provided for A3 printing and A4 printing. The PDF files named 'A3 gameboard' can be printed on A3 paper or card (or taken to a local printer to print out and laminate), and the PDF files named 'A4 gameboard' are split onto two A4 pages - you can print these out on A4 paper or card, trim and tape the two halves together to make the A3 games. We recommend you use a colour inkjet printer with photo-quality card to get the best results when printing these games.

Game cards - The first page of each set of cards is the colour reverse side for each sheet. Print from page 2 onwards then turn the paper or card over, reinsert into the printer and print page 1 onto the back of each sheet of cards.

Other game elements - Other elements, such as the decision cube, are included for some of the games and can be printed on A4 card.

Reflection sheets - The reflection sheets are to be printed on A4 paper to make up individul booklets for pupils.

The file directory on the CD is as follows:

Game folder	Folder contents
Bliss	A3 gameboard.pdf, A4 gameboard.pdf, Bliss Cards (Beauty).pdf, Bliss Cards (Interest).pdf, Bliss Cards (Love).pdf, Bliss Cards (Social).pdf, Bliss Cards (Spirit).pdf, Bliss reflection sheets.pdf, Blissbomb Cards.pdf
Cops and Robbers	A3 gameboard.pdf, A4 gameboard.pdf, Cops and Robbers reflection sheets.pdf, Cops Cards.pdf, Robbers Cards.pdf, Values Cards.pdf
FishBowl	A3 gameboard.pdf, A4 gameboard.pdf, Feedback Cards.pdf, FishBowl Cards.pdf, FishBowl reflection sheets.pdf, Fish Food Cards.pdf
Friendly Friends	A3 gameboard.pdf, A4 gameboard.pdf, Friendly Friends reflection sheets.pdf, Friendship cards.pdf, Friendship Challenge.pdf, Little Friend Tokens.pdf
Tease	A3 gameboard.pdf, A4 gameboard.pdf, Hint Cards.pdf, Money Cards. pdf, Pests and Bullies reflection sheets.pdf, Tease Cards.pdf
The Scariest Thing	A3 gameboard.pdf, A4 gameboard.pdf, Bravery Award Cards.pdf, The Scariest Thing reflection sheets.pdf, Tricks and Spells Cards.pdf
Think Again	A3 gameboard.pdf, A4 gameboard.pdf, Calm Cards.pdf, Decision Cube.pdf, Money Cards.pdf, Spinner.pdf, Think Again reflection sheets. pdf, What If Cards.pdf

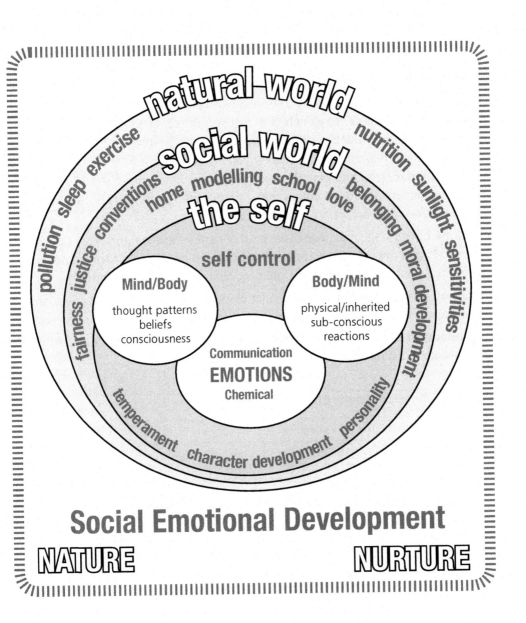

natural world

social world

the self

pollution sleep exercise

nutrition sunlight sensitivities

fairness justice conventions

home modelling school love

belonging moral development

self control

Mind/Body

thought patterns
beliefs
consciousness

Body/Mind

physical/inherited
sub-conscious
reactions

Communication

EMOTIONS

Chemical

temperament character development personality

Social Emotional Development

NATURE

NURTURE

Chapter One

Emotional Development

Emotional development is a dynamic process in which social, moral, biological, psychological and spiritual aspects of life have a role to play. For most children, this complex interplay leads to a good understanding of social conventions, moral issues and self-regulation. For those exposed to risks such as poverty and violence, resilience is enhanced by 'wrap around' services that provide strong support for families and schools and skill development in children. Research shows that teaching, modelling and coaching increase emotional literacy and compensate for temperamental disposition and social disadvantage (Bandura, 1986; Goldstein et al., 1998; Kagan, 1998; Karoly et al, 1998). Without assistance, children and young people who lack self-regulation face a life long disability, with ostracism from mainstream schools too often a feature. Clearly, early intervention is essential to avoid the many negative aspects of poor emotional development.

Emotions

Molecules of emotion

Emotions are the feelings we experience and interpret when neuropeptides, the 'biochemicals of emotion', are released in response to stimuli, both internal and external. According to Candace Pert, Professor of Physiology and Biophysics at Georgetown University, emotion is the glue that holds body and mind together (2001). Put simply, peptides and receptors create a communication network that runs every system of the 'bodymind'. Pert explains how mind becomes body through a multidirectional flow of information throughout the whole organism and how the body is the actual manifestation of the mind, and inseparable. Recent scientific discoveries like these raise implications for the connections between emotions and physical, psychological and social wellbeing. Pert makes the following suggestions based on her work:

▸ Become aware of mental, emotional, physical states operating at a subconscious level.

▸ Get in touch with the body – breathe, meditate, relax, visualise, have massages, spinal adjustments and hugs to strengthen the body's autonomic systems. Listen to music, practice mindfulness. Live in a state of personal integrity.

- ▶ Be aware of past experiences stored in the receptors of your cells. Release blockages with touch therapies, counselling, hypnotherapy, personal growth, meditation and prayer.

- ▶ Enter the bodymind's conversation in order to redirect it with helpful words and concepts – challenge negative thoughts – respond to what is occurring in the present.

- ▶ Reduce stress. Exercise – get the blood pumping to nourish and cleanse brain and body.

- ▶ Eat wisely, when hungry, in nice environs. Be conscious while eating. Avoid sugar.

- ▶ Tap into dreams to hear what the body and mind are saying about emotions and thoughts. They are direct messages from the bodymind.

- ▶ Avoid substance abuse.

Positive and negative emotion

Recently, scientists have been taking a closer look at how positive emotions affect us. Barbara Fredrickson, a psychology professor at the University of Michigan posits that positive emotions build enduring personal resources – physical, intellectual, social and psychological – in her 'broaden-and-build' theory of positive emotions (2002). These resources, in turn, function as reserves that can be drawn on later to help people survive and thrive. Negative emotions – fear, anger, and disgust – narrow momentary thought-action repertoires toward specific ancestral actions that promote survival. Positive emotions – joy, interest, contentment, love, pride, and gratitude – broaden momentary thought-action repertoires which also ultimately serve survival. This is the focus of the recently emerging science of positive psychology (Linley and Joseph, 2003).

Emotional development

Infancy and childhood

The first emotional bond occurs between mother and infant and extends to other members of the family and community during childhood. Infants who receive nurturing and unconditional acceptance develop a positive working model of 'the self' and 'others'. The mother mediates between the infant and environmental frustrations and anxiety can be communicated to infants from mothers holding them. Brain chemistry patterns begin to develop during this close period in response to emotional crises. The next important step for the infant is the development of self-regulation in response to frustration and fear of the unfamiliar. Richard Tremblay, professor of paediatrics, psychiatry and psychology at the University of Montreal, quotes longitudinal studies that show people who don't learn to regulate physical aggression in the pre-school years are at highest risk of serious violent behaviour during adolescence and adulthood (2004). It is usual for young children to use physical aggression when frustrated, until about the age of 30 months after birth, then levels decrease steadily until around five or six years old. Interestingly, verbal aggression peaks around six or seven years of age. Tremblay concludes that children have to learn not to use physical aggression in response to frustration. Over the first three years of life they learn ways to manage negative emotions, regulate attention, and comply with social rules by observing the models in their immediate world. Depending on the norms in their family and community, they witness a range of reactions to frustration – anger and hostility or self-calming and helpful self-talk – on which to model their own responses.

Tremblay says policies that maintain peaceful environments throughout society prevent 'primitive' aggressive reactions from breaking through the 'thin layer of civility' we acquire as we develop. People often fall back on aggression when no other options are apparent. Restorative justice and life space interviews help generate alternatives to aggression. Families, schools, communities, mass media all have important roles to play during these formative years.

Adolescence

Adolescence is a time of great physical, social, cognitive and emotional change. Teenagers are managing a confusing array of social and moral issues while the body and brain are still developing. It is a time of cognitive development that allows reflection on values and the different aspects of the self within a background of personal and cultural environments. Normal adolescent fears centre on failure and social dysfunction. Important issues to adolescents are looking good, being independent of parents, winning and being part of a peer based social group. At the same time, identities are being formed and 'heroes' or models in the social world are emulated, including the sometimes troublesome examples provided by popular media. It is an important time for adults to support young people as they navigate the confusing messages coming from a multitude of sources to cope with frustration and anxiety. Adolescents need skills such as help-seeking, distraction, interpreting, self-calming, delaying gratification, controlling the environment, expressing emotion and exercising the body.

Adolescents with emotional difficulties are often addressing unresolved developmental anxieties from earlier stages of life or dealing with emerging psychiatric disorders that have been passed on genetically. Unsupported, they can create hard veneers that are difficult to break through. Unconditional positive regard, consistency, skill development, guided practice and recognition are needed from parents, teachers and coaches. When interventions are not working, assessment and treatment by a child psychiatrist is essential.

Social environments

Emotion is vital to social communication and the ability to manage emotions is an important predictor of social and academic success (Halberstadt et al., 2001; Keltner and Haidt, 2001; Zins, et al., 2004). Children learn about the complex structures of society through observation, play and relationships and it can take some time for them to discover the arbitrary nature of the conventions in their social worlds (Nucci, 1997). Social conventions and cultures organise and co-ordinate interactions within social systems and these shared, uniform behaviours are determined by the social systems in which they are formed. Manners and civilities are like 'social oil' that helps relationships run smoothly. Schools are particularly skilled in maintaining the status quo of these conventions, at times with mindless adherence to tradition without considering the worth of individual practices. Successful social skills programmes are contextual and integrated into all aspects of school, including manners, civilities, cooperation, perspective-taking, conflict resolution and emotional control.

Research reveals a positive relationship between the ability to manage emotions and the quality of social interactions (Lopes et al., 2003). As a society, each individual provides sample behaviours for young people to consider. The words we use and attitudes we hold provide a 'scaffold' for the thought constructs and belief systems that they may choose to use when resolving emotional problems (Vygotsky, 1976, 1986). Children learn about managing emotions from watching models in their social world, including the mass media, and through play experiences with peers (Connolly et al., 1988). Social disadvantage can also affect behaviour and emotional development.

Moral development

Justice, fairness and compassion are at the heart of moral development and are common issues at the core of crises faced by children and young people. Attempts to direct the emotional development of children must not suppress or eliminate emotion as this stifles emotional control and moral development (Mayer and Salovey, 1997; Salovey and Mayer, 1990). Children as young as three years old are able to discern the difference between moral issues and social conventions. According to Nucci (1987) young children make judgements that show an understanding of fairness versus social convention and this ability is evident across cultures. Preschoolers can state that hitting someone would be wrong even if there were no rules against it whereas running in the playground would be fine if there were no rule. Naturally, children start with an egocentric perspective on moral dilemmas but understanding moves towards reciprocity, and eventually, special consideration for disadvantaged groups as development occurs.

Moral education goes hand in hand with social and emotional development. Approaches that use, for example, philosophic inquiry, 'transactive discussion' (Berkowitz, 1982), moral dilemmas, literature and open-ended discussion of immediate social issues, help young people develop a meaningful set of values, beliefs and attitudes. Exhortation to do good and recitation of moral virtues at best leads to thoughtless conformity and at worst, robs young people of the opportunity to cultivate autonomy and self-determination (Kohn, 1997). Presentation of awards, certificates, trophies and other tokens of recognition for virtuous behaviour where some children are singled out as winners has the unintended effect of disrupting relationships (in order to be a winner) and lessening commitment to being virtuous.

Genetics and the environment

Genetic make-up influences physical characteristics and temperament and people are born with predispositions to many conditions, including anxiety, shyness, aggression and depression. These different temperaments are attributed to varying thresholds for circuit activations within the brain (Gowen and Nebrig, 2002). Genetics influence the development of other psychiatric disorders such as bi-polar disorder and schizophrenia which usually emerge during adolescence.

At the same time, emotions are sensitive to environmental factors such as nutrition, sunlight, sleep, exercise, laughter, fun, water, pollution, relationships and relaxation. Take nutrition for example. According to Dr Alex Richardson (2004), senior researcher at Oxford University's physiology laboratory and co-director of the Food and Behaviour Research group, we are what we eat and what we eat has changed hugely over the past 50 years. The physical risks to children of a highly processed, highly refined diet lacking in fruit and vegetables are now acknowledged, but the damage being done to their behaviour, learning abilities and mood is not. Werbach and Moss (1999) identify nutritional deficiencies (thiamine, magnesium, niacin, vitamin B6, vitamin C, iron, amino acids) and exposure to heavy metals (cadmium, lead) as contributors to aggressive behaviour.

Spiritual development

The 'bodymind' human is a network of energies driven by psychological and physical factors within social and natural worlds. Some say the driver of this vehicle is in our spirit. Spiritual understandings influence the motivation to accept responsibility and learn self-control. While difficult to explain, spirit refers to ideals and morals, to religious practice, to the 'flavours' of our interactions with others (for example, caring, grateful, jealous or negative spirits). Research into adolescent development shows that greater levels of religious or spiritual practice lead to better mental health outcomes (Wong et al, 2006). The important issue with emotional development is that it is an evolving process and when young people realise this, they can be encouraged to strive for their ideals, even in the face of failure and disappointment. As we scaffold learning environments (emotional, physical, social, academic, moral and spiritual) children are supported as they learn the skills to succeed and to deal with disappointment. The 'honourable self' flourishes in young people in communities where values, beliefs and attitudes reflect fairness, justice and caring in the decisions that are made. We all are teaching – all the time.

Resilience

Resilience refers to the multidimensional, dynamic process of positive adaptation to adversity. It is the ability to 'bounce back' from adversity and change and involves internal and external adjustments to risks such as poverty, parental mental illness, maltreatment, discrimination and trauma (Butler, 1997; Hawley and DeHaan, 1996; McGrath and Noble, 2003; Walsh, 1996). Fundamental to resilience are strong relationships within family and social contexts (Luthar, 2005). Individual characteristics, such as intact central nervous systems, intelligence, self-motivation, sociability, autonomy and being good at 'something' are protective internal factors. External protective factors include 'good enough' attachments, physical needs met, education, clear boundaries, leadership and other opportunities for meaningful participation (Werner and Smith, 1982). Genetic and biological influences have a protective role to play as well, but it is the positive engagement in the interpersonal world that most predicts resilience in young people. A protective social network for example, guards a child against victimisation or the ill effects of a learning difficulty. For children from chaotic backgrounds this role is often filled by a teacher, counsellor, mentor, coach or other member of the community.

Long-term, positive relationships help young people develop a sense of identity, and with mastery, the 'honourable' or ideal self grows. Academic success, positive relationships and healthy physical development are all important for the development of emotional resilience.

Protective individual characteristics

- pleasant temperament
- social intelligence
- sense of belonging
- sense of self-efficacy
- sense of humour
- work success as an adolescent
- a gift or talent
- high intelligence
- take criticism constructively
- intact central nervous system.

Protective family factors

- at least one warm relationship with a parent or carer
- a sense of belonging and connection with family
- having qualities the family values
- consistency, continuity.

Peer and adult support that is protective of children

- positive early school experience
- connection to school, community
- achievement of academic goals
- positive relationship with peers, adults
- someone who believes in them.

INTERNAL RISK FACTORS

- Impulsivity, inattention, hyperactivity
- Anxiety, depression
- Poor self-esteem or inappropriately high self-esteem
- Poor relationships with family and peers
- Heightened perception of hostile intent in others
- Low frustration tolerance.

STRESSORS

- Maslow's hierarchy of unmet need
- Stress response – fight flight
- Communication difficulties
- Environmental irritations
- Developmental stages
- Social / family
- Abuse.

DEVELOPMENTAL ANXIETIES

- Abandonment 0-2 yrs
- Inadequacy 2-6 yrs
- Guilt 6-9 yrs
- Conflict 9-12 yrs
- Identity adolescence.

Emotional Crises

Attack: self/others - REACTIONS - Withdraw: depression/drugs

emotional first aid – IMMEDIATE RESPONSE – life space interview

avoid punishment – shame – anger – violence cycles

classrooms **UNIVERSAL** emotional literacy
teach - model - values - morals

small groups **TARGETTED** specific issues
teach - coach

family **CLINICAL** child
special education
psychological
medical

TEACH

- BodyMind connection
- Emotional first aid
- Problem solving
- Values/Morals
- Social skills
- Optimism.

STRATEGIES

- Attention vs detention
- Coaching/Counselling
- Lunchtime programmes
- Restorative practice
- Therapeutic games
- Stop-Think-Do
- Circle Time
- Parent training.

EFFECTIVE LONG TERM RESPONSES

- Dynamic, flexible, cultural, policies, structures
- Early intervention across family, school, community, medical
- No blame, emotional literacy, restorative practices, quality pedagogy.

Chapter Two

Emotional Difficulties

Challenge is vital to child development; the body grows in response to physical challenge, courage grows in the face of disappointment and moral development is sharpened by social injustice. But excessive stress causes damage, sometimes permanently. Extreme poverty, child abuse, neglect, homelessness, parental mental illness, genetic inheritance, organic syndromes and family dysfunction impact on the growing brain and an over-reactive physiology is set in place. Resilience develops in response to stress and challenge, but children who are already stressed by social or emotional disadvantage may lack the self-regulation and social skills needed to cope in healthy ways. An assessment of these stressors will identify areas requiring attention, adjustment, accommodation or modification. Stressors which may increase a child's risk for emotional problems include:

- family stress, such as a move, job loss or birth of a baby
- chronic sickness or medical condition in the child or another family member
- grief and loss caused by death, parental separation or divorce
- remarriage and step-parenting
- exposure to violence, either within or outside the family
- foster care
- frustration with schoolwork
- peer pressures.

Over recent times there has been a shift in focus from the medical or 'internal to the child' model when considering emotional and behavioural difficulties, to a community/school based model of intervention where an holistic approach is taken (Cooper et al., 1994).With early intervention, eco-systemic approaches reduce exposure to adversity by supporting children and their families with educational, medical and social interventions. This chapter explores some of the reasons for the development of emotional difficulties and the nature of effective interventions for children with mild to moderate emotional difficulties.

Developmental anxieties and stressors

A range of anxieties develop as the result of unmet emotional needs. Children need nurture, comfort, unconditional acceptance, skill development, mastery, independent experience, adult approval and success in new situations to develop a positive sense of self. When these basic emotional needs are not met, disabilities develop and children exhibit behaviour that is 'stuck' at earlier developmental stages. For example, a teenager who is reluctant to try new things and says, 'I can't do it,' is likely to be dealing with issues of inadequacy. The following table shows the hierarchy of developmental anxieties which provides a framework for understanding the emotional needs of children and possible reasons for the difficult behaviours that develop in response to unmet needs (in Wood and Long, 1991). The table helps devise immediate and long term responses to emotional crises. In the case of the 'inadequate teenager' above, her behaviours represent quite a moderate emotional disability. Her anxieties around success and mastery may be resolved by adult approval, skill development, and problem-solving skills, assuming her physical, social and learning needs are addressed too, of course.

If unresolved	Developmental anxiety	Resolved by
Annihilation of self, stealing, hording, superficial attachment.	**Abandonment** (0-2 y/o) Catch-cry: 'No-one cares.' Needs: nurture, care, security.	Unconditional acceptance, comfort, security, consistent care.
Fear of the unknown, self doubt, blaming, denial.	**Inadequacy** (2-6 y/o) Catch-cry: 'I can't do it.' Needs: success, mastery.	Adult approval, skill development, problem- solving.
Self-deprecation, unworthiness, outrageous behaviour.	**Guilt** (6-9 y/o) Catch-cry: 'I'm a loser.' Needs: mental, physical and social skills.	Success, adult sanction, independent experience.
Defiance, aggression, manipulation, peers versus adults.	**Conflict** (9-12 y/o) Catch-cry: 'Try and make me.' Needs: shift from external to internal regulation.	Learning that freedom has responsibility.
Self-doubt, defensiveness, experimentation.	**Identity** (adolescence) Catch-cry: 'Who am I?' Needs: identity formation, independence, responsibility.	Success in new situations, recognition, personality formation.

Developmental stressors

Stressors external to the control of the child may impact on emotional development. Environmental, social and communication factors form a background of stress which makes coping in prosocial ways difficult for some young people. Following are potential stressors to consider when looking to understand and remediate emotional difficulties:

Maslow's hierarchy of unmet needs

▶ survival – physical needs such as food, water and air

▶ security – resources, family, safety, health

▶ love and belonging – families, friends, partners, groups

▶ self-esteem – respect and recognition

> ▶ self-actualisation – growth toward human potential, the moral stance of fairness, justice and compassion.

Environmental irritants/circumstances

> ▶ physical – heat, lights, noise, sounds, crowds

> ▶ lack of structure and planning at home and/or school

> ▶ lack of positive adult roles models at home and/or school.

Communication difficulties

> ▶ expressive/receptive language disorders leading to poor self-concept, poor frustration tolerance, stigmatisation and sometimes violence

> ▶ withdrawn response style – nonverbal – self-harm and isolation

> ▶ passive responses – whining, blaming, being a victim

> ▶ aggressive responses – verbal, blaming, hostile, loud, glaring

> ▶ assaultive responses – hitting, kicking, injurious behaviour.

Antisocial behaviour and aggression

While the reasons for antisocial behaviour are multiple, research into aggression identifies a variety of traits and indicators amongst which are: impulsivity, inattention, hyperactivity, anxiousness, depression, low self-esteem, inappropriately high self-esteem, troubled relationships with parents and perception of hostile intent in other people's neutral statements (Bower, 1998). Some of these traits are inherited (nature) while others are products of our social environments (nurture). Other factors, such as abuse and violent TV, also impact on aggression and antisocial behaviour. Research into violent TV and video games also reveals increased violent and aggressive behaviour, increased high-risk behaviours (alcohol and tobacco use) and early onset of sexual activity (Villani, 2001).

According to Goleman (1995), brutality and cruelty to children leaves a clear mark on their brain chemistry. Abused children are often quick to anger and typically have low levels of serotonin, a neurotransmitter that inhibits aggression. Evidence is mounting that combinations of syndromes, head injuries and child abuse lead to brain dysfunction. Something is 'physically wrong' and it impedes the ability to play by the rules of society (Gladwell, 1997). In chronic situations, the biomolecular system in young brains becomes programmed to response-sets of agitation and aggression, making behaviour management in large classes difficult. Gladwell refers to the work of Dr Dorothy Lewis, a psychiatrist at New York's Bellevue Hospital, and Jonathan Pincus, professor of neurobiology at Yale University, which suggests that some aggressive children have a genetic predisposition to lower serotonin and heightened dopamine levels in the brain. When environmental factors are also adverse, these children are prone to aggression.

Aggressiveness presents a difficult situation to schools. On the one hand, children with emotional difficulties need to be managed with compassion and wisdom, while on the other hand, schools cannot condone behaviours such as bullying, taunting, fighting and violence. In fact, the Occupational Health and Safety policies in most workplaces demand risk assessments and management strategies for young people with a history of violence. A child with a quick temper is at the mercy of many factors – biological, social, emotional – and they need respectful and patient attitudes to develop appropriate skills. At the same time, firm boundaries are needed around aggressive behaviour, while avoiding the pitfalls of punishment, shame and humiliation. Opportunities for restitution and skill development should be provided within a climate of encouragement and recognition of progress. Young people with severe difficulties require intense, educational interventions that include specialist medical and psychological treatment and possible special education placement.

Criticism and the shame-anger-violence cycle

When attachments to significant others are poor, the growth of personal identity is disrupted (Gerhardt, 2004). Criticism leads to feelings of low self-worth and fuels the shame-anger-violence cycle (Nathanson, 2003; Riches, 1998). Tomkins (1991) describes nine separate 'affects' or feeling states people experience at different times. He describes the affect shame as an inner sense of inferiority or failure in comparison with others on issues of size, strength, skill, independence, competitiveness, defectiveness, personal attractiveness, sexuality, lovability, and in some extreme cases, just being 'seen'. When young people receive messages of high worth and respect, they experience the positive 'social self' feelings of pride and self-respect. Conversely, messages of low self-worth and disrespect lead to feelings of shame and inferiority which, if left unresolved, turn to rage and violence.

For vulnerable young people, any perceived slight against their sense of self is met with furious defence and attack of others. For some, the alternative is to live diminished, self-destructive lives, avoiding the sense of shame through drugs, withdrawal or self-mutilation. Tomkins (1991) and Nathanson (2003) describe how the experience of shame at a time when young people are reflecting on who they are 'becoming' can be so painful they build defences against it. Some defences to shame are damaging to the self and others:

- attacking others, put downs, physical assaults, aggressive attitudes
- diminishing life by withdrawing, being a victim, fearing what others think, depression
- attacking the self, self-harm, sense of defectiveness, self-hatred
- avoidance through drugs, sex, plastic surgery, superficiality, high risk taking.

For some young people, the 'fight-flight' reaction becomes an almost immediate, physiological response to frustration, competition, humiliation and perceived threat. Young people are often caught in a shame-anger-violence cycle which is further perpetuated by punishment, humiliation and a lack of understanding. Shame strikes deep into the heart and anger and aggression are too often the result. At a time when characters are forming and young people are working out who they are becoming and how they fit in to the world, self-concept can be fragile. Young people need protection from the ill effects of punishment, criticism and misguided discipline.

Effective interventions

Effective interventions are dynamic, flexible and culturally specific strategies that aim to reduce risk, develop academic, social and physical competence and scaffold support around young people. We know from research that effective interventions start early in primary school, use problem-solving rather than punitive approaches, gain whole-school commitment to policies and structures, and use peer-based, protective and supportive programmes (Rigby, 2002). It is vital for these approaches to be embedded within the organisational structures of a school to develop a strong culture of support and respect. This means:

- policies that ensure safe schools are well-known and consistently applied
- social and emotional literacy is included the curricula
- opportunities are provided for moral development and values clarification in the classroom
- there is respect for difference
- there are opportunities for fun – positive playground programmes, peer leadership, peer mediation, peer support
- bystanders are empowered to 'watch out' for each other and to seek help when needed

- ▶ help-seeking becomes an accepted part of the school culture.

- ▶ listening to young people and responding quickly to reports of teasing or bullying

- ▶ no blame, restorative practices are used (Maines and Robinson, 1997; McCold, 2002; O'Connell and McCold, 2004).

- ▶ there is ongoing skill development – communication, problem-solving, help-seeking, self-calming.

Early intervention

Early intervention is the key to good outcomes for children from disadvantaged backgrounds and there is wide support for the effectiveness of such programmes in terms of life outcomes for young people and economic considerations (Berhman, 1995; Karoly et al., 1998; Perry, 1996). Governments are beginning to lend support to structures that bring together community agencies such as education, social services, health and housing in an intervention model to support families with young children. Examples include: Families First NSW, Australia; Sure Start United Kingdom; Ireland National Children's Plan; HeadStart USA.

Re-conceptualising schools

Early intervention into the lives of 'at risk' children is essential in stemming the tide of youth violence; however, children at risk arrive at school without contact with early intervention programmes (Walker et al., 1996). Walker et al re-conceptualise the role of schools in preventing antisocial behaviour among children and youth, seeing schools as:

- ▶ co-ordinators of schools, families, social service agencies, medical clinics

- ▶ implementers of fair policies and practices that are known to children and young people

- ▶ providers of universal approaches to reduce risk factors and enhance protective factors

- ▶ meeting the needs of 'at risk' children early with remedial programmes instead of exclusionary practices.

The Fast Track Project (2006) is an example of an early intervention programme that commences when children enter school. It is a comprehensive, multi-site intervention designed to prevent serious and chronic antisocial behaviour in children selected as high-risk at school entry because of their conduct problems in kindergarten and at home. The Fast Track project is based on the hypothesis that improving child competencies, parenting effectiveness, school context, and school-home communications will, over time, contribute to preventing antisocial behaviour. The project has been running in four diverse communities in the USA since 1990 and evaluations show moderate to substantial positive outcomes for young people in the projects (Conduct Problems Prevention Research Group, 2002).

Universal, targeted and clinical responses

According to Reid (1993), the adjustment problems of 75 to 85 percent of children are resolved with well-implemented primary prevention (universal) programmes executed at the classroom level. Targeted programmes focus on children deemed to be at risk of disadvantage through small group programmes addressing specific academic, social and emotional skills. At the tertiary level, young people with significant emotional difficulties receive intensive, individual, multi-agency case management approaches. Successful interventions which operate at the universal, targeted and educational levels include:

Universal programmes

- ▸ school policies and practices that provide safe and happy environments
- ▸ emotional literacy in the classroom – Circle Time (Roffey, 2006)
- ▸ guided discussion of social and moral dilemmas (Kohn, 1997, Nucci, 1997)
- ▸ opportunities for children to develop leadership qualities (Blum, 2000)
- ▸ classroom practice that is fair, firm and flexible (Nucci, 1987)
- ▸ monitoring the playground and data collection (Hromek, 2004)
- ▸ proactive, fun playground activities (Hromek, 2004)
- ▸ restorative practices (McCold, 2002; O'Connell and McCold, 2004).

Targeted programmes

- ▸ emotional first-aid – allowing time and space for cooling off, anticipating problem situations (Greene, 2001)
- ▸ talking therapies for defusing a crisis – Life Space Interview (Redl, 1966, Wood and Long, 1991)
- ▸ direct teaching of social skills, anger management strategies and moral reasoning in small groups (Goldstein, 1998)

▸ therapeutic games (Hromek, 2005)

▸ emotional coaching.

Clinical programmes

▸ co-ordinating interventions across different settings (Stoolmiller et al., 2000)

▸ solution-focused, strength-based approaches to working with schools and families (Durant 1995)

▸ close monitoring through case management

▸ individual behaviour programmes

▸ intense language, academic, emotional skill development programmes

▸ special education settings

▸ medical intervention, child psychiatry.

Managing students with emotional difficulties in the classroom

Whole-school policies that are consistent in providing security for young people and that have clear directions, purpose and expectations are fundamental to a positive school experience. Within this background, classes that meet the learning needs of the student are essential. A strong association exists between poor academic attainment and maladjustment. Teaching that is motivational, engaging and meaningful is the most effective means of preventing antisocial behaviour (Fitzsimons-Lovett, 2001). Young people with emotional difficulties benefit from the security of firm, fair and flexible teachers who are prepared to try a range of strategies until they find the most effective way of managing their behaviour (Jordan, 1997).

Emotional Coaching

Future oriented – transformational – goal based relationship
Increases academic achievement, social relationships, self-concept and goal achievement
Reduces rates of recidivism, substance abuse and aggression.

COACH

- Emotionally intelligent
- Understand child developmnt
- Communication skills
- Willing to talk about feelings
- Optimistic, encouraging, fair
- Empathic, dependable
- Teachers, aides, counsellors
- parents, mentors, peers.

ISSUES
Anger
Anxiety
Happiness
Friendships
Depression
Teasing
School

YOUNG PERSON

- Ability to listen
- Ability to reason
- Willing to trust
- Willing to set goals
- Commitment to effort
- Willing to do their best .

Process

- meet regularly
- set goals
- practice strategies
- provide feedback
- track progress, rewards
- life space interview
- involve parents teachers.

Relationship

- conversational style
- positive, optimistic
- fun based
- Teach / model, skills
- respect boundaries
- medium to long term
- philosophical.

Chapter Three

Emotional Coaching

Supportive relationships with 'non-parent' adults can powerfully influence the course and quality of young people's lives. Research shows that relationships with at least one positive adult role-model are essential to youth's health and wellbeing, especially for highly stressed young people (Benson et al., 1998; Rutter and Giller, 1983). Mentoring relationships positively influence academic achievement, relationships, self-concept and career and personal goals. Attendance at school increases, recidivism rates, substance abuse and physical aggression are reduced in juvenile delinquents who have been mentored (Davidson and Redner, 1998; Grossman and Tierney, 1998; McPartland and Nettles, 1991; Reisner et al., 1998). A meta-analysis of mentoring programmes by Dubois et al (2002) shows favourable effects across diverse programmes. Practices associated with stronger effects include infrastructure features such as screening, support and training for mentors, structured activities, frequent contact, parental involvement, and monitoring of programmes. The longer the commitment made to mentoring, the greater the benefits (Rhodes, 2002). It is important to be clear from the beginning about the specific aims and structure of the programme and the time limits imposed on it. Rhodes (2002) identifies the characteristics that potentially work against effective programmes:

- ▶ unrealistic expectations, rescue fantasies
- ▶ lack of time and commitment
- ▶ overwhelming 'painful memories' triggered
- ▶ lack of connection between particular coaches and students
- ▶ lack of 'rewards' or satisfaction for coach and student
- ▶ inability of the young person to develop trust – vulnerability to loss
- ▶ unclear parameters including beginning and end-points, frequency of contact
- ▶ lack of training or support for coaches.

Emotional coaching

Emotional coaching refers specifically to skill development around emotional issues. Coaching is a future oriented, transformational process where coach and young person work together to reach goals important for wellbeing. Coaching is neither counselling, nor discipline. It is a structured relationship that encourages young people to take action and to develop competence in social and emotional skills in a safe and supportive environment. Emotional coaching should be part of wider, eco-systemic interventions that involve families, schools, social networks, and when necessary, medical and other therapeutic agencies. 'Natural' coaching relationships occur within schools, families and communities and seem to offer certain safeguards around support for the coach and student. Coming from the natural environment they have greater opportunity to see the young person's strengths and understand their background, and are more likely to have sustained long term ties. These more natural coaching relationships exist between young people and teachers, heads (principals), counsellors, psychologists, extended family members and community workers. Skilled educationalists and psychologists will need little training in order to use the programme presented here. Volunteers without a background in education or psychology will need training, ongoing support and monitoring.

This book presents a philosophical and encouraging style for working with children while learning cognitive behavioural strategies and developing emotional first-aid plans. Games and reflection sheets provide the opportunity for guided practice of these and other skills. Emotional crises are debriefed using a life space interview and restorative practices are used to resolve these events. Emotional crises are viewed as opportunities to explore morals, values, consequences, restitution and ways of behaving that maintain the young person's dignity. Working with parents, carers, teachers and young people to create a common language and understanding means that crises are dealt with in consistently respectful and fair ways, thus preserving the positive self-concept of the child.

Children and young people

These resources are intended for individual or small groups of children and young people with mild to moderate emotional difficulties. The basic requirements for a young person to engage in coaching include:

- ▶ the ability to listen

- ▶ a basic understanding of words – ability to describe things

- ▶ ability to reason

- ▶ willingness to trust an adult

- ▶ understanding of what constitutes a coaching relationship

- willingness to meet with their coach and create goals

- commitment to effort

- agreement to do their best.

Children with severe emotional difficulties may also benefit from learning about their emotions but other interventions and accommodations are required to fully support them. While it is true that the negative impact of life stressors in some individuals may limit emotional control, most will benefit from coaching, especially if they are under the care of a child psychiatrist and their moods have been stabilised by medication.

The coach

Coaches are emotionally intelligent individuals who are interested in the development of children and willing to commit to medium to long term involvement with them. They understand the importance of relationships and the physiology behind emotion. They read the physical and cognitive signs of different emotional states in children and have a repertoire of socio-emotional skills to model. They are aware of their own emotional states and how to manage their feelings. Emotional coaches:

- like children and are prepared to get to know their interests and worries

- have good communication skills and express warmth and acceptance

- understand child development, have realistic, positive expectations and believe children are a 'work in progress'

- have good self-regulation skills and are willing to talk about feelings

- motivate children through encouragement – instill a love of learning

- help young people to stop procrastinating and to persist when tasks get hard

- know how to use emotional first-aid and the life space interview

- give constructive criticism that is limited to what needs to be done and not directed at the personality of the young person

- help children develop goals and plans and celebrate successes

- are empathic, objective, dependable, fair, respectful, curious, philosophic

- teachers, parents, carers, counsellors, aides, principals, mentors, peer leaders psychologists, community members, older adults, volunteers.

Training and support for coaches

Coaches with a background in education, psychology or other 'helping' professions have the advantage of pre-existing skills and knowledge about child development. Volunteer coaches without this background should be screened through written applications, personal interviews, reference checks and criminal record inquiries. Their training should focus on building trust, child development, ethical issues, teamwork and skill development. Support networks should be set up for coaches that meet regularly to provide training, support and debriefing. The background reading, games and reflection sheets in this book can be used to provide a basic understanding of the psychological content required for emotional coaching.

Ethical issues	clear boundaries – simple rules limits to what can be achieved through coaching trust and the limits to confidentiality rewards and motivation the importance of commitment self-disclosure – what to tell child protection – dealing with disclosures from children how to finish a coaching relationship.
Teamwork	case management issues positive feedback to families, teachers when to refer for specialist assessment importance of ongoing support, debriefing and training.
Skill development	understanding child and adolescent development holding conversations – language, eye level – interests, concerns encouraging children to talk reflective listening – 'That sounds scary. What did you do? open-ended questions – 'How do you feel about that?' social skills, civilities – modelling, guided practice encouragement, specific praise –helpful words and phrases managing difficult behaviour – distraction, emotional first-aid things to avoid – preaching, being judgemental, asking why, prying, dismissing feelings, belittling, over-involvement.

The coaching relationship

Coaching is a positive, collaborative relationship relying on a reflective, conversational style of interaction. A curious, philosophic, optimistic attitude is maintained towards the young person and emotional crises are explored with respect. The relationship:

- ▸ is encouraging, non-disciplinarian
- ▸ medium to long term – three to nine months or more
- ▸ is strength building – courage, interpersonal skill, rationality, insight, optimism, perspective, capacity for pleasure, meaningful life
- ▸ uses strengths-based, future-oriented, solution-focused, problem-solving approaches
- ▸ includes parents, teachers as supports for reaching goals and using new strategies
- ▸ is reflective – data and reports from home and school are collected to map progress
- ▸ is celebratory – broadcasting success to parents, teachers and others
- ▸ has appropriate boundaries.

When coaches are part of the student's everyday school world, for example, head teachers, deputies, SENCos, etc, they are able to be an immediate support if emotional crises occur. When coaches are not in the immediate environment, life space interviews can be used to debrief the incident at the next meeting. In this case it is important that other supportive adults in the immediate environment encourage the young person to use their emotional first-aid plans when crises occur.

The coaching process

Emotional coaching may be part of a wider, long term mentoring programme or as a specific, time limited strategy to help young people develop emotional control around specific issues. Sessions last for about thirty to forty minutes per week. Coaching sessions aim to:

- ▸ set goals for emotional and behavioural control – discuss the range of consequences of not developing emotional control
- ▸ teach about the body's physiological responses to emotion, the effect thoughts have on emotion, cognitive restructuring, relaxation techniques, guided imagery

- ▶ identify the body's early warning signals for feelings of anger, anxiety, depression – tight fists, chest, shoulders or throat, feelings in the stomach, legs or head

- ▶ determine 'fuse-length' to angry reactions – how long between when first feel anger in the body and when no longer able to think straight – become aggressive

- ▶ identify strengths and strategies that already work for the young person – develop an emotional first-aid plan

- ▶ teach a range of skills – making friends, managing feelings (anxiety, anger, depression) physical, cognitive, communication and life style adjustments

- ▶ empathise with feelings and motives while supporting limits placed around behaviour by schools and families – allow natural and logical consequences to occur

- ▶ apply emotional first-aid when emotional crises occur

- ▶ debrief emotional crises using the life space interview

- ▶ use therapeutic games and reflection sheets to practice skills

- ▶ review progress regularly – obtain accurate feed-back about how the child is going in other settings – reset goals – encourage persistence

- ▶ work with parents, carers and teachers – inform them of the strategies being used

- ▶ create optimism through recognition and broadcasting of success

- ▶ refer to a child psychologist or psychiatrist if interventions are not working.

Rewards and motivation

The issues of reward and motivation are linked to social and moral development and deserve careful consideration. External rewards come from outside the child, for example, gifts, certificates and privileges. Intrinsic rewards are less tangible, longer-lasting and more pervasive. They are the thoughts, feelings and meanings we make to feel good when we are satisfied, for example, thinking you did a task well; having a smile to yourself; taking a deep breath, noticing beauty, etc. are rewards we give to ourselves. Studies have found the more you reward people for doing something, the more they lose interest in whatever they had to do to get the (external) reward (Kohn, 1993). It is possible for young people to misinterpret external rewards or for coaches to misuse them. Being open and up-front about why we are using a reward system guards against a focus on the reward by the young person. The spirit in which the reward is offered is important, for example, a spirit of gratitude – 'Thank you for your hard work this week – let's celebrate' – is less likely to be problematic than the more manipulative approach – 'If you go to school this week you can have that new toy you've been wanting'. Rewards should be natural, positive consequences for achieving goals.

While keeping these concerns in mind, external rewards can be used in a transient way to help anxious and angry children break negative cycles and take control of their feelings. Some young people will benefit from gimmicks and games which inject fun into their work and help them focus on their goals. Charts and stickers can 'jump start' motivation and map tangible proof of effort and progress. Some young people need visual aids to help them see the connection between sticking to a plan and reaching their goals. Charts and stickers are usually only effective for about three or four weeks during which time children can be encouraged to find internal motivations for their reaching their goals. Once success is gained and goals are being met, reliance on external rewards reduces naturally and the child's internal reward system takes over as the basis of their motivation and will.

Kohn (1993) suggests that alternative strategies to rewards and punishments should include:

- ▶ look at what is being asked of the young person – take into account its meaning or value to the young person

- ▶ engage the child in how to accomplish the task

- ▶ work with them to reach their goals.

In this approach the child is encouraged to think about why things are important, how to solve problems and to take ownership of the solution, making it more likely to succeed. This deeper, more challenging strategy involves bringing the young person into the problem-solving process and inviting them to take responsibility for who they are becoming. Authentic choice, active participation, games of chance and creative 'sillinesses' keep children motivated in the process. Gradually, motivation is sustained by the confidence which grows from skill development and the satisfaction gained from self-mastery. Our work as coaches, parents and educators is to create the conditions where self-motivation flourishes and to help young people understand how persistence brings reward.

When to seek professional help

In general, when a student has not made progress over the course of three or four weeks, the family should be advised to contact their doctor and discuss the need for assessment and treatment by a child psychiatrist. Ongoing signs or symptoms to be aware of include:

▸ Problems listening or behaving

▸ Excessive activity (hyperactivity)

▸ Difficulty concentrating

▸ Ongoing difficulty with friends and other children

▸ Chronic sadness, irritability or grumpiness

▸ Difficulty sleeping or excessive sleeping

▸ Eating disorder (eating too much or too little)

▸ Frequent worrying and fearfulness

▸ Extreme shyness

▸ Continued reluctance to attend school

▸ Suicidal thoughts

▸ Substance abuse

▸ Aggressive and/or risky behaviour

▸ Sudden change in behaviour or school performance.

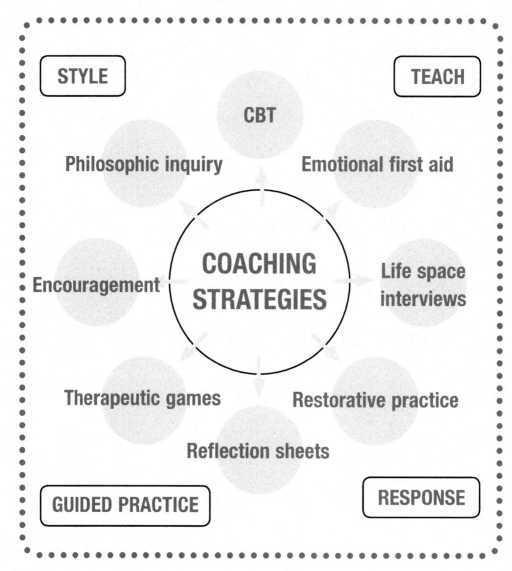

Chapter Four

Coaching Strategies

This chapter provides a range of strategies to use while coaching young people around social and emotional difficulties. These strategies reflect a philosophical and encouraging style of interaction while teaching young people the skills of cognitive behavioural therapy and emotional first-aid. Therapeutic games and reflection sheets provide an opportunity for guided practice in a safe environment. Life space interviews and restorative practices provide respectful ways of dealing with emotional crises when they occur.

Philosophic inquiry

Philosophy is the love of wisdom. Philosophy seeks the truth about 'reality' through reason and argument, draws conclusions based on facts and challenges the foundations of beliefs, a teaching for which Socrates died. Socrates called on his pupils to question beliefs and their underlying assumptions as an antidote to prejudice, fear and social conditioning. Philosophy helps people think about things that are important to them from different points of view. It helps people make decisions about how they might live in society, in the natural world, and indeed the universe. Philosophic inquiry involves:

- Questioning, for example, Is it fair to suspend violent children from school?

- Gathering information – How wide spread is the practice of suspension? Who is it protecting? What is the effect on the person suspended? What alternatives might there be? When does this rule not apply? What do other people think? What has been my experience? What would happen if they weren't suspended?

- Reasoning – What is the evidence? What is fair and just? What makes sense? Consider several points of view.

- Forming conclusions – What makes the best sense to me? What are my beliefs and attitudes? What is my conclusion about the question? Why?

- Defending conclusions – What are the reasons for understanding the issue this way? What supports my point of view? What are alternative points of view?

Encouragement

To encourage is to inspire with confidence, hope and courage. Encouragement draws attention to the effort, persistence and skill brought to challenges and builds a store of positive self-concept by reference to actual accomplishments and effort. Positive statements by adults have a powerful impact on children and young people (Thomas, 1991). When giving specific praise use the child's name and avoid general comments such as 'good boy' or 'well done'.

Encouraging statements:

- ▶ 'I understand how you feel. I'm sure you'll handle it like you did before.'

- ▶ 'It's a good feeling when you reach one of your goals – good for you.'

Specific praise:

- ▶ 'You did a good job of avoiding trouble with Tim this week.'

- ▶ 'I like the way you are willing to try new things.'

Encouraging young people to talk:

- ▶ 'You look a bit sad today. Would you like to talk about it?'

- ▶ 'Wow – that sounds scary. What did you do?'

Cognitive behavioural therapy

Cognitive behavioural therapy (CBT) focuses on the mind and its thinking patterns. From ancient times words have been thought to have power and influence over what people do and feel. Words are like 'information processors' that help make sense of things and depending on the point of view of the thinker, they come with a pre-existing cluster of meanings. Think of the phrase 'she's a victim of teasing' compared to 'she's a target of teasing'. Notice the connotations of suffering that go with the word 'victim' and the degree of freedom afforded the 'target' to dodge the teases. And so a 'world view' forms and mindsets develop, both helpful and unhelpful. By thinking about thinking, CBT makes one aware of the power of the word and the possibility of changing habitually negative thinking patterns.

People with negative thinking patterns tend to exaggerate, jump to conclusions, expect perfection and catastrophise their circumstances. It seems the subconscious mind (body) is listening when we say negative things about ourselves such as 'I'm so stupid'. A spiral of not trying, lost experience, poor skill development and loss of self-esteem leads to shame, humiliation and aggression or withdrawal. Fortunately it seems we can learn new habits of mind and behaviour. According to Pert (2001), our bodies are our subconscious minds and open to suggestions, especially at times of relaxation and guided imagery. Pert uses the term 'psychosomatic wellness' to describe the process of guiding our 'selves' into states of wellbeing through thoughts, words and actions.

CBT has proven to be protective of psychological wellbeing (Kendall, 1994; Montgomery and Evans, 1984). Cognitive restructuring is the process of catching negative thoughts, challenging them with logic and substituting helpful thoughts. New understandings develop when strengths are identified and helpful words used. Scripts or mantras can help with self-calming. Scripts need to be realistic and specific and based on previous positive experience to be effective, for example, 'I can handle this – I have handled it before,' and, 'As I slow my breathing I begin to feel calmer'.

Emotional first-aid

Emotional first-aid (EFA) recognises that emotion is based on physiological reactions in the body involving neuropeptide releases that have a course to run, sometimes taking up to 20 minutes to dissipate. EFA uses strategies that allow time and space for self-calming to occur. Work out individual EFA plans in advance so when emotional crises occur, a common language exists to guide the self-calming process. During a flood of emotion:

▸ use a soft, calm, 'matter-of-fact' voice
▸ keep verbal directives and comments to a minimum
▸ give them time and space to follow their EFA plan
▸ be aware of your 'buttons' – things that arouse strong emotions in you
▸ recognise if you have entered a power-conflict cycle and disengage.

Step 1 Assess physical and cognitive states. Identify risks to the child, yourself and others. If there is danger of attack, allow time and space to calm down. Look for the following:

Physical symptoms	Cognitive symptoms
▸ red, sweaty face	▸ shouting
▸ short breath	▸ swearing
▸ wide eyes, frowning looks	▸ angry words
▸ agitated and aggressive actions.	▸ irrational thinking.

Step 2 Encourage the young person to use their EFA plan. Use reflective listening to help dissipate feelings. Listen for rational talk as they calm down.

Physical self-calming strategies

▸ Drink water – wash face – cool down.

▸ Walk or run – allow time for things to calm.

▸ Slow the breath – take even breaths to maintain oxygen / carbon dioxide balance and reduce feelings of panic. Count 1, 2, 3, in – 1, 2, 3, out.

▸ Some children prefer to sit alone for a while to calm down – in the sun, on a comfortable chair, somewhere private.

Helpful things to say

▸ Self-calming statements – 'Relax, let go – its not worth losing it'.

▸ Confidence building – 'You can work this out – take time to calm down'.

Reflective listening

Reflective listening validates the young person's feelings and helps engage them in a conversation about gaining control.

▸ Say back the content of what the child says.

▸ Say what you think the child is feeling.

▸ Show you understand the child's point of view, validate their feelings and the values they are upholding.

Step 3 Re-assess the emotional state. When agitated activity calms down and the young person starts to use rational words to talk about their experience, they can be engaged in a life space interview. It may be necessary to re-apply EFA if the child struggles to cope. If the young person has not calmed down after about 20 minutes, debrief the crisis at a later time. Ensure the safety and dignity of the child and others at all times.

Therapeutic games

Therapeutic games take advantage of the natural inclination of children and young people to play (Hromek, 2005). Call something a game and everyone wants to play. Rapport is quickly established and discussions of therapeutic issues arise in a fun, semi-structured way. Playing therapeutic games with a skilled game leader provides the opportunity for modelling and guided practice of new skills in a safe environment. Basic teaching points around a range of social and emotional issues are embedded into the cards and game boards. Chance and fun make it an enjoyable experience for young people. Invite a small group of friends to play as well. Teach the main psychological concepts while explaining the rules and at selected points during the game. Work out some basic rules with the players, for example, listening, waiting, saying nice things. Keep things balanced between talking and playing. Provide opportunities for behaviour rehearsal and thinking about thinking.

Reflection sheets and mindmaps

The reflections sheets provided with this resource offer a way of summarising the main teaching points and assessing progress. The reflection sheets use mindmaps, drawings, lists and charts and are designed to engage young people in discussion about the challenges they are facing and planning their responses. With current learning styles shifting from the auditory twentieth century styles to an emphasis on visual learning, these reflection sheets are in line with most children's preferred learning styles. Children with emotional difficulties often have reading and writing problems and prefer schematic presentations of information. Personalise reflection sheets with colour, highlighters, arrows, words, ideas etc. The reflection sheets can also be used to share information with parents, carers and teachers.

Mindmaps are visual presentations that encapsulate concepts being explored through colour, shape and relationship to each other on the page (McGregor, 1992). They are a great way to organise information gained from brainstorming ideas and as a study guide to help with thinking and learning. The diagrams at the beginning of every chapter are examples of mindmaps, as are most of the reflection sheets. Following is an example of how to use a mindmap.

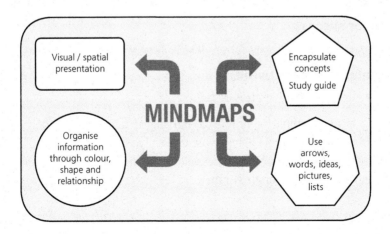

The Life Space Interview

The Life Space Interview (LSI) is a verbal technique for working with children in crisis where reactions are used to expand understanding of their behaviour and the responses of others (Redl, 1966; Wood and Long, 1991). The coach assists in defusing and decoding feelings behind actions and identifies values and central issues. For example, emotional crises often develop around perceived violations of fairness. A young person who defends their mother's honour from another's curses is responding to a firmly held sense of justice, and rightly so. The difficulty arises for the young person when they choose to respond with physical and verbal violence. By acknowledging the worth of the value they are defending and their motivations, coaches show deep understanding of where the young person is coming from. Trust develops and a sense of relief is experienced by the child who is then in a better place psychologically to enter the problem-solving phase of the interview. Alternative behaviours and acts of restitution are explored and a plan is chosen. Preparations are made for re-entry to normal activities by rehearsing responses, accepting consequences and exploring 'what ifs'.

Steps of a Life Space Interview

1. **Emotional first-aid**

   Words – breath   TIME – SPACE   water – activity

2. **Focus on the incident**

   Talk – listen   REFLECT   clarify – understand

3. **Indentify values, central issues, goals**

   DIGNITY – developmental anxieties – goals

4. **Problem-solving and restitution**

   Brainstorm options – evaluate consequences – restitution – CHOOSE

5. **Plan for success**

   Rehearse – anticipate reactions – ACCEPT consequences

6. **Re-enter normal activities**

   CALM – responsible – matter of fact.

Following is an example of how a coach might use a LSI to debrief their student about an incident. Tim is an eleven year old boy who has been working with a coach for one month. Last week Tim swore at another student and made verbal threats against him.

Step 1: Use emotional first-aid to establish an empathic connection

Assess emotional state – allow time and space when emotion is flooding. Suggest calming strategies from the EFA plan. Identify and empathise with feelings. This step ends when rational words are used to communicate.

Coach: Hi Tim, how are things going this week?

Tim: OK – I got angry with James last week.

Coach: I heard about that – you seem a bit disappointed.

Tim: Yeah – stupid James – he's always saying stupid things.

Coach: And you're still angry about it – is it OK to keep talking about it now?

Tim: Yeah – it's OK – Mr Simons helped us sort it out.

Step 2: Focus on the incident

Use reflective listening to gather facts, validate feelings and maintain rapport. This step ends when time, place and people are identified and emotional intensity is lowered.

Coach: So what happened last week?

Tim: Stupid James was following me around the playground calling my mother some bad names – so I chased him and said I'd punch his head in.

Coach: Tim, I have to ask you to stop calling James names – we treat each other with respect here. So you felt angry when he wouldn't stop calling your mother names. Remember how we have been working out your body's early warning signs? I'm curious about how your body felt at the time?

Tim: I don't know – I just remember getting mad – I felt like punching him

Coach: Congratulations on your decision not to punch him. A few months ago you might have tried to hurt James. So did you feel it in your fists?

Tim: Yeah – I wanted to smash him but I didn't.

Step 3: Values, central issues and therapeutic goals

Identify motives, values and central issues behind the actions. This step demonstrates deep understanding and prevents shame-anger-violence cycles. This step ends when issues have been stated concisely and therapeutic goals are chosen. The teacher identifies anger management as the central issues and problem-solving as the immediate goal. The value was respect for his mother. His mistake was defending her honour with aggression and threats.

Coach: I'm really curious about how you were able to do that – I mean not smash him. How were you able to manage your anger so well?

Tim: I thought about what might happen. I didn't want to get suspended.

Coach: I'm impressed. You felt angry but you were able to manage without violence. I can see why you were angry. Saying mean things is disrespectful to your mother and against our school rules. But from what I hear, your verbal threats towards James were pretty scary.

Tim: I just wanted to teach him a lesson.

Coach: James does need to be more respectful. Mr Simons has been helping him with this. What could you do if this happens again?

Step 4: Problem-solving, alternative, consequences and restitution

Options, consequences and acts of restitution are explored and plans are made. Because the debriefing occurred some time after the event, mediators had helped create a plan and acts of restitution had been applied.

Coach: What are the kinds of things you could say or do if it happens again?

Tim: I could say, 'Don't worry about it,' but I do worry about it.

Coach: Yes, I understand that – maybe remind yourself that Mr Simons is helping. Get a drink of water and think 'calm down – I can manage this'. What do you think of that?

Tim: It sounds OK.

Coach: You told me about a time when someone teased you and you walked away to get a drink – so it works for you sometimes. How are things between you and James now?

Tim: Mr Simons told us to go to peer mediation. We worked out a plan where he doesn't say bad things and we stay away from each other. We both said sorry. But I still don't like him.

Coach: You don't have to like James, you just have to be polite. How are you feeling about all of this now?

Tim: I feel OK I guess. I shouldn't have chased him, it got me into trouble.

Step 5: Plan for success

Strategies are rehearsed and the reactions of others are anticipated, 'what ifs....' are explored. This step ends when the young person knows how to handle the current issue and future events.

Coach: So what if James comes up next week and starts mouthing off again?

Tim: I'll tell him to be quiet and if he keeps going, I'll see Mr Simons.

Coach: Sounds like a good idea. What if Mr Simons isn't at school that day?

Tim: I don't know – maybe go to the office – or the playground teacher.

Coach: OK. What if you feel your fists getting tight – what will you do then?

Tim: I'll go off and get a drink of water or sit somewhere quiet to work it out.

Coach: Sounds good. It's OK to feel angry, but it's not OK to hurt others. What does your mother say to you about James?

Tim: She says don't worry about it, but it isn't fair if he gets away with it.

Coach: No, it isn't, but Mr Simons is helping with this.

Tim: Yes, he has been helping me. James hasn't said anything since then.

Step 6: Re-enter normal activities

Because this scenario was a debriefing session and not dealing with an immediate crisis, this phase would simply be a statement along the lines of:

Coach: That all seems to be going well then, Tim. Congratulations. So what shall we do for the next 15 minutes? Play a game?

Restorative practice

Restorative practice allows open, transparent, honest and fair ways of relating and resolving conflict (McCold, 2002; O'Connell and McCold, 2004). It addresses harm done to others while maintaining relationships. Young people are invited to take responsibility for their actions by acknowledging the harm caused and finding ways of repairing damage to property or relationship. Restitution is an important way to build relationships and improve self-concept. When children see things from the other person's point of view, empathy develops and a desire to make amends grows. A new self-concept develops of being someone who is able to make amends for mistakes. This face-saving device releases the child from the futile grip of guilt, giving them the psychological space to understand the repercussions of their actions. Children should be encouraged, not forced to engage in acts of restitution and to choose what to do in consultation with the target of their actions, as appropriate. Acts as simple as apologising are acceptable, as are offers to fix things, letters of apology or attending remedial programmes. Questions that reflect restorative practice:

'What were you thinking at the time of the incident?'

'What have you thought about it since?'

'Who has been affected by what you have done?'

'What has been the hardest thing for you?'

'What do you think you need to do to make things right?'

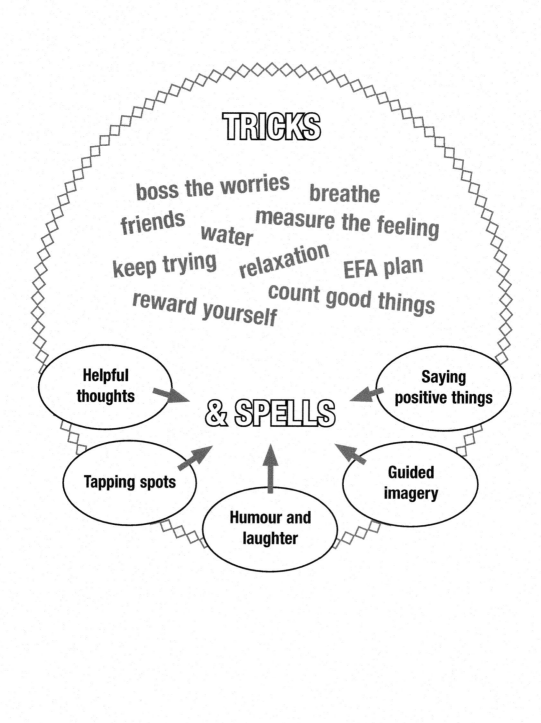

Chapter Five

Tricks and Spells for Kids

Watch your thoughts . . . . for they become words

Choose your words . . . . for they become actions

Understand your actions . . . . for they become habits

Study your habits . . . . for they become your character

Develop your character . . . . for it becomes your destiny.

Anonymous

Tricks and spells are used in this book as metaphors for the thoughts, words and actions we say and do. Sometimes they are positive and helpful and sometimes not. This chapter sets out simple effective strategies for young people to use to help calm the self and gain emotional control. The ideas put forward are a mix of cognitive behavioural strategies and energy therapies. Among the 'tricks' are emotional first aid, relaxation, guided imagery, slow breathing, identification of feelings, gratitude and mindfulness. The 'spells' refer to helpful thoughts, positive words, humour, laughter and tapping spots (Emotional Freedom Technique).

Tricks

Emotional first-aid plan

An emotional first-aid (EFA) plan is worked out with the young person at a calm time and in anticipation of future emotional difficulties. EFA plans analyse the challenges being faced, identify early warning signs of anger or anxiety, then work out things to say and do when unpleasant feelings come. This plan is recorded and the steps are rehearsed in anticipation of challenging situations. Evaluation of the EFA is ongoing in order to find the best options. Include self-calming strategies such as slow breathing, walking away to get a drink water, calm self-talk, assertive communication or seeking supportive people. The reflections sheets for Chapters Seven and Nine contain ideas and formats for setting up an EFA.

Identifying early warning signs is an important part of an EFA plan. When we are upset, the body produces neuropeptides which are felt in the body as increased heart rate, rapid breathing, headache, sweating etc.. These physical sensations can be used as early warning signs for the need to calm down. The trick is to notice these feelings and use them to remind us to create time and space for them to dissipate. We need to use self-calming strategies such as relaxation, breathing and thinking straight when we are becoming upset to help us calm down. The 'felt sense' exercise below is a way of helping young people identify where in their bodies they are feeling these sensations. Early warning signs are also able to be used as 'tapping spots' in the emotional freedom strategy below.

Relaxation and guided imagery

Studies confirm the effectiveness of relaxation and guided imagery in dealing with anxiety and depression (Bennett and Disbrow, 1999). Guided imagery uses the power of imagination as a potent healer. Imagery can relieve physical and emotional pain, speed healing and help the body subdue all kinds of ailments. While in a relaxed state, guided imagery can strengthen emotional control by recalling or describing times when the young person was brave, strong, having fun, etc.. The following exercises are brief versions of relaxation techniques which, with practice, can be used to stimulate the relaxation response at other times, for example, while waiting for a test.

Students sit in a comfortable chair or lie on their backs on the floor. Use a script similar to the following to make suggestions in a calming voice. Afterwards, talk about the experience. Ask what they saw, what creatures, what smells, colours, etc. came to mind. Some young people do not easily imagine a safe place. Help them identify somewhere pleasant they have visited or seen in a book. If they say they can't think of anywhere then suggest they just imagine it. Suggest that they imagine this safe place and tap their early warning spot while taking a deep breath and thinking the word 'relax'.

Physical release

We are going to practice letting our bodies relax while taking some deep breaths and imagining a calm, safe place. Firstly, give yourself permission to relax and close your eyes take a deep breath in and as you breath out, think relax...notice where your body is touching the chair or the floor...feel yourself sinking into the chair or floor...as you take your next deep breath, tighten the muscles in your legs and feet...hold them tight...and as you breath out, let your muscles go and think relax...as you take your next deep breath, tighten the muscles on your back and tummy...hold them tight...and as you breathe out, let your muscles go and think relax...as you take your next breath, tighten the muscles in your shoulders and arms...hold them tight...and as you breath out, let your muscles go and think relax...

Guided imagery

(Continue on from the above script)

Continue to take nice even breaths as you listen to the noises around you... listen to the (clock, birds, footsteps, trees, cars, voices)...now listen to my voice...take a deep breath and as you breath out think relax...now listen to the (birds, footsteps, trees, etc...alternate listening to the different sounds with listening to your voice – all the while taking deep breaths and thinking relax on exhalation)...While you are feeling relaxed, gently tap on your bodies early warning spot (previously identified) as you take another deep breath... breathe out and think relax...Now listen to my voice and as I count from 10 to 1, imagine going down some steps leading to somewhere beautiful, safe and calm...10...9...8...7...6...5...4...3...2...1...some people imagine they are walking along a path in the forest with flowers and little creatures playing among the trees...some like to imagine a warm day at the beach with gentle waves rolling onto the sand...or a lovely garden with birds and butterflies...or a sunny room in a comfortable house...as you continue to breathe evenly in and evenly out, look around where you are...what colours do you see...look up - what is above you...the sun...clouds...tree tops...what can you smell?... the earth...flowers...salt air...find a comfortable spot in your imaginary safe place and lie back...breathe in and tap your early warning spot while you remember this place...you can visit this place anytime in your imagination and remember to relax...if you are upset, tap your spot and remember this safe place and the feeling of being relaxed...now it is time to come back into this room...slowly as I count from 10 to 1, imagine that you are leaving your safe place 10...9...8...7...6...become aware of the noises around you again ...5...4...3...feel your body and wriggle your toes...2...1...back in the room... have a stretch and when you are ready, open your eyes.

Slow breathing

This strategy acknowledges the body's quest for homeostasis, its constant attempts to keep the body's mechanisms in balance. In some cultures breath is known as the source of the life force. The in-breath and the out-breath carry oxygen and carbon dioxide into and out of the body and when this is out of balance a feeling of panic develops. If feelings of panic or anxiety are being experienced, equalizing the breath reduces the feeling. Counting breath in and out is meditative and when combined with walking, the emotions settle. This exercise can be practised while in a relaxed state (created above) or while walking or sitting in a chair.

...breath in and out slowly – count 1...2...3...in 1...2...3...out 1...2...3...in 1...2...3...out 1...2...3...in 1...2...3...out. We can count our breath when we feel scared, such as when we're waiting to make a speech, or when we feel upset - such as when someone is mean...or when we are running or exercising...

Felt sense

People experience emotions in a range of locations around the body; in the neck, shoulders, fists, knees, stomach, chest, headache, etc. Some young people are unable to identify where they experience emotions, so this exercise is a way of putting them in touch with their feelings. Invite them to visualise a series of vignettes and to notice how they feel in each one and where they experience this feeling in their body. Talk about where the feelings were and whether the different emotions were felt in different places. Being aware of where the feelings are allows them to be used as early warning signs. These spots, that is, the chest, neck, head, hands, etc., can be used as tapping spots in emotional freedom technique (EFT).

(Begin with the physical relaxation exercise above.)

While you are feeling relaxed, I am going to describe a scene for you...take a deep breath in and imagine you are at school and standing in line to buy some lunch...your feeling very hungry...notice where you feel the hunger... now imagine someone rudely pushes you out of the line...now how do you feel...where in your body do you feel this feeling...take a deep breath and let the feeling go...deep breath in and deep breath out...relax...now imagine you are in the school assembly...all your friends are there and everyone is excited...suddenly you hear your name being called out...you have to go to the front of assembly to receive an award...how do you feel now...where do you feel this...take a deep breath and let the feeling go...deep breath in and deep breath out...relax...now imagine you are left out of a game at school... all your friends are playing except you...now how do you feel...where do you feel this...take a deep breath and let the feeling go...deep breath in and deep breath out...relax...now it's time to come back into this room...start to listen to the noises around you...feel where your body is touching the floor or chair...deep breath in and deep breath out...think the word relax...when you are ready, stretch and open your eyes.

Measure the feelings

This exercise externalises the feelings being felt and can give children a sense of control as they see the size of their feelings reduce. Children who experience anxiety can usually show how 'big' the feeling is in their stomach aches or headaches. Have them move their hands apart to show how big the feeling is and measure this with a ruler. Enter the measurement onto a chart to watch how things change over time. Charting progress is usually effective for about three or four weeks, by which time the young people will have learnt new ways of dealing with angry or scary feelings.

Boss of the worries

Worries are unpleasant, unhelpful thoughts that keep coming back. Usually something is wrong and there are problems to solve. This is how to become boss of the worries:

- ▶ Write down the worries – one per page.

- ▶ Work out some solutions, pick the best ideas. Find someone to help if necessary.

- ▶ Tell the worries you are not going to think about them anymore today but you will make a time to think about them again later, for example 6pm.

- ▶ When the time comes, get out the pages and think of more solutions – add new ideas.

- ▶ Put the pages away after five or ten minutes – tell the worries that time is up.

- ▶ Make another appointment to think about your worries if you need to.

- ▶ Go and do something else – something you are interesting in.

Floating worries

Relax and imagine your thoughts floating away like a cloud. See them going up in a hot air balloon. Imagine they are trains going into a tunnel. Write them down and put them away. Wrap them around a rock and carry them in your bag – the heavier the rock the better (!). Throw them away when you are finished with them. These and other funny silliness are a good strategy.

Gratitude – count the good

We show gratitude by learning to love what is, which naturally leads to loving actions. Gratitude doesn't change the events in our lives but it does alter the way in which we view them. Gratitude and other positive emotions enhance individual growth and resilience, can reconcile relationships and can spread through other group members to increase optimal social and communal wellbeing. Cultivating gratitude has been found to undo the effects of negative emotions such as anger and anxiety (Fredrickson, 2002). In a research study of college students, those in a group who kept gratitude lists reported having more energy, fewer health problems and a greater feeling of wellbeing after three weeks than those who complained or gloated.

When we stop and appreciate the good things in our lives; the beauty, the loves, friends and meaningful pursuits, our bodies release 'anti-stress' neuropeptides, such as endorphin. When we pause to enjoy the perfume of a rose or the palette of a sunset, we regain the openness that is an essential part of gratitude. Children need to learn about the tactile joys of flowers, plants, crayons, paint, music and dancing. Writing thank you notes or keeping a notebook or scrapbook are ways of reminding ourselves about the good things in life. We develop more positive outlooks on life as we collect a store of goodness to remember at difficult times. Learn about authentic happiness by playing BLISS (Chapter Twelve).

Mindfulness

Mindfulness meditation is designed to enhance wellness in people with emotional difficulties such as depression, anxiety, chronic pain, stress and eating disorders. Research shows mindfulness training reduces relapse rates in depression (Miller et al., 1995; Segal et al., 2002). Mindfulness aims to enhance awareness of the 'wandering of the mind' and to use this awareness to manage emotional states more effectively. The breath acts as an anchor point while cognitive challenging and attention refocusing strategies bring the practice into conjunction with cognitive behavioural strategies. Mindfulness is a living, meditative activity that young people can learn to use with practice.

Mindfulness is the practice whereby a person is intentionally aware of his or her thoughts and actions in the present moment, non-judgmentally. It is applied to both bodily actions and the mind's own thoughts and feelings. For example, one strategy is to mentally give a verbal label to the position of the body whenever it changes. When one is sitting, one thinks of the word 'sitting', when standing up, one thinks 'standing up', when walking, one thinks 'walking'. Using breath as the primary focus of attention, the meditator applies the process of 'participatory observation' to all of the perceptions. One's own mental activities and the fluctuations of consciousness itself are studied. The practice of mindfulness is similar to the relaxation and guided imagery exercises above and is particularly helpful at times of anxiety, panic and pain.

Spells

Helpful thoughts and positive words

At the basis of cognitive behavioural therapy is the notion that thoughts can be unreasonable and negatively influence the way we feel about situations. Young people can learn to replace negative thought patterns with positive, helpful scripts. As a first step, negative feelings need validation before clearing them and creating positive scripts. When children feel they have been understood, they then have a choice to continue to perceive their situation as negative or choose to change their thoughts and words into more helpful ones. Children stuck in negative thought patterns can use EFT to help unblock negative thinking patterns and feelings. When helping young people create scripts:

▸ decide what will be helpful

▸ use positive words and phrases, for example, 'I choose to feel positive....'

▸ use words that are specific, descriptive

▸ make scripts short and simple

▸ start scripts with, 'I am...,' 'I have...,' 'I can...'

▸ embed therapeutic suggestions, for example, 'I feel calm when I go for drink of water.'

Humour and laughter

Humour is a universal language. It's a contagious emotion and a natural diversion making it an excellent way to deal with negative emotions and difficult situations. It brings other people in and breaks down barriers. Best of all it is free and has no known side-effects. Patients, doctors and health-care professionals are finding that laughter may indeed be the best medicine. Laughter lowers blood pressure, reduces stress hormones, increases muscle flexion, and boosts immune function by raising levels of T-cells and B-cells, the disease-destroying antibodies. Laughter also triggers the release of endorphins, the body's natural painkiller, and produces a general sense of wellbeing.

Young people can learn to use nonsarcastic humour and unexpected reactions to divert attention or diffuse explosive situations. Humour can be used when issues are not all that important and situations need to be cooled down. Important issues will need to be addressed at a time of calmness with respect for all parties involved paramount. Laughing at these times can give the wrong impression. By way of reminder: laughing is a common nervous reaction of children to stressful events and adults must take care not to misinterpret this natural response.

Emotional freedom technique

Emotional freedom technique (EFT) is based on the idea that energy flows around the body along acupuncture meridian lines. Sometimes, according to the theory, these pathways get blocked by negative emotion causing anxiety, phobias and even physical illnesses. The EFT technique involves gently tapping meridian points with the fingertips while focusing on the negative emotion and repeating positive scripts. A scientifically controlled study on EFT at Curtin University in Western Australia found a single 30-minute treatment session of EFT could produce valid behavioural and subjective effects on phobias (Wells et al., 2003).

A simple adaptation of EFT is to tap early warning spots while repeating a positive statement. The early warning spots are the places in our bodies that first show we are feeling anxious, angry or scared, for example, the chest, neck, shoulders (identified in 'Think Again' and 'Scariest Thing'). If children cannot identify these spots, they can use the meridian on the top of their heads as a tapping spot. Create scripts that relate to the emotional difficulty:

- ▶ Even though I am scared I completely accept myself.
- ▶ When I am scared at school I remember my emotional first-aid plan.
- ▶ When I get angry I remember my emotional first-aid plan.
- ▶ I am kind and respectful to my friends.
- ▶ I am thankful for the support and love of my family.

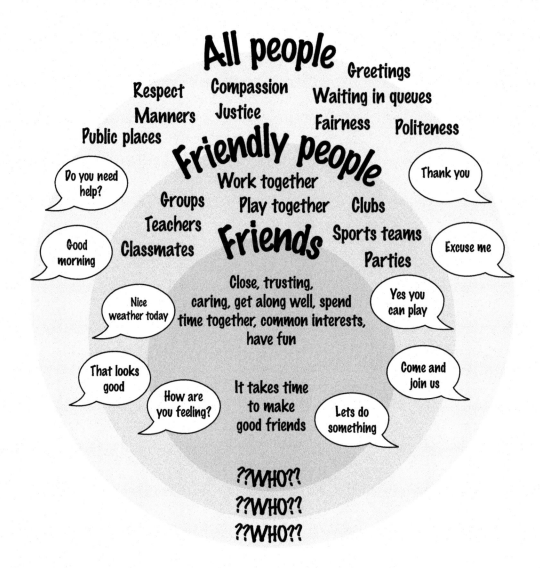

Friendship

Chapter Six

Friendships

Childhood friendships can be a joy and delight or a source of heartache and pain. Yet socialising is the most important issue to kids at school – just ask them – and rightly so. Good relationships are vital to resilience, wellbeing and growth; productivity goes up, sorrows are eased, zest and energy increases. Children who are rejected by their peer group or fail to develop close friendships are at risk for depression, anxiety, and low self-esteem as adults. Children's friendships are the training grounds for important adult relationships. It is in relation to others that we understand ourselves best and learn to manage our emotions and develop communication skills to maintain successful relationships. Qualities such as courage, forgiveness, and kindness develop as we meet challenges, make mistakes and need comfort. It helps to view friendships in the context of developmental stages and within a framework of wider relationships we have with the people we work and play with and the wider community as well.

Social development in general and friendship in particular are linked to moral reasoning and cognitive development. For example, skills such as empathy do not emerge until the child develops a 'theory of mind', that is, an understanding that other people have minds and feelings. Temperamental dispositions also impact on the ability to make and keep friends. Individuals with cheerful, co-operative and outgoing temperaments have less trouble making and keeping friends than fearful, shy and retiring individuals. There are sex-based differences too. In the younger years there is a natural tendency towards same sex relationships. Girls seem to develop more intense, longer lasting relationships with a few other children than do boys and more likely to exclude others from their circle of friends as they grow older. Boys may have intense friendships with one or two other boys but also have wider friendship groups that change and shift rapidly. There are developmental stages too. Selman (1981) sets out the characteristics and skills of friendships across ages of three to fifteen years old. At each stage a different set of challenges are faced with a new set of developing skills.

Age range	Characteristics	Skills
3 – 5 years old	Momentary encounters, recognition, parallel play.	Meshing, coordinating conversations, self-regulation.
4 – 9 years old	Self-oriented relationships, friends valued by what can be gained, change often.	Emerging skills – the ability to encode and decode emotion appropriately.
9 – 12 years old	Two-way relationships, 'Fair weather' friends – mistakes attributed to deliberate intent, peer influence growing, cliques developing.	Meshing of conversations – body language, social distance, eye-contact. Repairing relationships. Character development.
9-15 years old	Reciprocity – friendship valued because it is mutually rewarding and intimate.	Trust, empathy, mutual support. Ability to identify emotion behind words.

Circles of relationship

In broad terms, people engage each other at three levels: most broadly, a universal level that recognises human rights for all; next, a level of friendliness that is offered to those with whom we work and play; and more intimately, a level that is close and supportive.

Universal level of relationship

This is the level of ethical duty to society. At this level, a set of social conventions, civilities, moral obligations and human rights are determined by society and expected by all citizens. At school this means being polite to everyone, even people not liked or who have been mean in the past. It means using 'manners' when making requests or responding, using greetings and acknowledging the rights of others. Public behaviours such as waiting in queues, sharing public space and accessing services require us to be fair and treat others with respect in order to produce harmonious interactions.

'Good morning.'	'Thank you.'
'Please.'	'Can I help you?'

Friendly relationships

The next level includes those with whom we work, play; relationships that are characterised by chatting, sharing jokes, eating lunch together and inviting each other to events. Children do not have to be 'friends' to play or work together, but being friendly helps them co-operate and reach common goals. Sometimes the significance of playing or working together can be misunderstood by young people and they can unnecessarily exclude people who are not friends from play. When they understand that they do not have to be friends to be friendly, children can be encouraged to include others, especially children new to school or social isolates. People at this level of relationship include staff, classmates, sports teams, working groups and playmates.

'Come and join us.'	'How are you going?'
'That looks good.'	'Nice weather today.'

Close relationships (friends and family)

People in the inner circle of friends have close, trusting and caring relationships where significant time is spent together and secrets or inner thoughts are shared. High quality friendships provide validation, intimacy and companionship. Friends tend to share similar characteristics, temperaments, interests and styles of play. As children grow, their needs and interests change, and so may their friendships. Friends should be chosen wisely since young people are vulnerable to peer pressure. Close friendships may become exclusionary and jealousies arise resulting in feelings of rejection and loss and some children may need help dealing with painful feelings. Children in close friendships should be encouraged to maintain friendly relationships with others and remember to invite them into their games.

'Let's do something together.'	'How are you feeling about that?'
'I need to talk to you about something.'	'Would you like to share this with me?'

It is a mistake to insist children become friends with those they do not like or with whom they have nothing in common. Friendships develop over time and are based on feelings and intuitions and cannot be forced. When children understand that they do not have to be 'friends' with everyone but that they are expected to be polite and friendly to the people they play and work with, it can help resolve some of the intense feelings around friendships. With this understanding, children tend to be more accepting of others and more likely to include social isolates or new children in games or work groups. Knowing that they don't have to be friends with everyone but that they do have to be polite and friendly releases them to work and play with a wider range of people at school. When friendships breakdown or do not form, there should be an expectation that children will treat each other with respect and dignity.

Successful friendships

It is good for children to mix in many social groups to learn who they are in relation to others and how to behave in different contexts, for example, school, sport, dance, arts, church, etc..

Making friends

Friendships are built on the willingness to participate, the ability to communicate and co-operate and on validation of each other in order to succeed. At a basic level, one needs to appear friendly and be accepting of others. There is a raft of micro-social skills that are necessary for success and most children learn these by observing the role-models in their social environments. Children who lack these skills can benefit from direct teaching that uses modelling, guided practice, social reinforcement and moral development. These skills include listening, responding, meshing conversations, body language, eye-contact, social distance, turn-taking, talking about interesting things, etc.. Qualities that support friendship include: loyalty, courage, tolerance, unselfishness, flexibility, playfulness, cheerfulness, humour, gratitude, cooperation, encouragement, optimism, resourcefulness, skillfulness, reliability, honesty, helpfulness and respect for peer conventions.

Emotional control

One of the most important skills for successful relationships is emotional control. Self-regulation is needed to deal with frustration, disappointment, teasing, competition and jealousy and feelings may need to be acknowledged and managed for relationships to be maintained. Losing gracefully, sharing, being kind, resisting negative peer pressure and taking advice are not well developed sometimes. Children can learn a range of self-calming strategies (going for a walk, drinking water, slow breathing, relaxation, tapping, guided imagery, positive self-talk) and how to read and manage the emotional states of others. While managing their internal emotional states, young people need to interpret and mesh with the emotional messages being sent to them in order to maintain relationship.

Repairing relationships

Conflict and misunderstandings inevitably occur and children need skills to be able to repair and their restore relationships. For this they need emotional control, communication skills and conflict resolution skills to negotiate with others. Perspective and empathy grows as children develop the ability to see things from the other person's point of view. When children are sorry for the harm they have caused, character is developed as they learn to apologise for mistakes and to forgive others for their mistakes. Wisdom develops as we learn from our mistakes. When relationships are irreparably damaged, those involved must treat each other politely even though trust may not develop again.

Dealing with rejection

Sometimes quite intense feelings of grief and loss develop around lost friendships. Rejected children can derive comfort from being heard, from problem-solving around why they lost their friends and how they can find new ones or repair their old relationships, for example, through mediation and development of friendship skills. Philosophic discussion about the nature of friendships and trust can help them decide if they really were true friends in the first place and encourage them to find friendship elsewhere. When a child is rejected by a clique of friends, it may be more realistic to help them develop and maintain one or two close friendships elsewhere. Even just one friend is protective.

Some rejected children lack positive interactions because they are not co-operative, helpful, or considerate toward others and instead are aggressive, mean, disruptive, bossy, withdrawn, apprehensive, dishonest, resistant, impulsive or insulting. Coaching in sports and games and how to be friendly will help them develop the skills of positive social interactions.

Young people who may benefit from this approach

The ideas and resources presented in this chapter are designed for young people aged six or seven years and up with relationship difficulties. Both the shy and withdrawn isolates and the bossy and impulsive extroverts will benefit from learning about relationships. The reflection sheets and game teach friendship skills and allow young people the opportunity to discuss and practice new skills. Young people who do not make gains over a few months may need assessment and treatment from a educational psychologist or child psychiatrist. Children who continue with domineering behaviours will need firm boundaries and close monitoring in social situations.

Coaching sessions

In your introduction explain how you will work together to learn some ways of making friends and being friendly. Maybe something along the lines of...

'I would like to talk with you about some ideas I have that make it fun to play with other kids. You can tell me which ideas you like and then try them out and let me know if they help make things more fun.'

Use the reflection sheets to teach about the three levels of relationships. Identify people who belong in each circle. Listen to children's experiences and identify the skills they need to learn in order to make friends – managing emotions, communication, cooperation, encouraging others and repairing relationships. Empathise with feelings of grief or loss from rejection by peers. Complete the questionnaire to identify strengths and skills that need building.

Invite a group of friends to play Friendly Friends (page 61). Choose social dilemmas from the cards that are relevant to the situation and age group. Hold philosophic discussions about the issues that arise. Reinforce good role-models. Talk to parents and carers about arranging play dates or structured activities such as sport and drama to provide opportunities for making friends. Review progress over the weeks and celebrate successes. Discuss your exit from close involvement when appropriate

Friendship – reflection sheets

Use the reflection sheets to teach friendship skills and monitor progress. Share the sheets with parents and teachers, where appropriate, to help generalise the strategies being taught. Use colour and words to personalise the reflection sheets.

Page 1: Friendship circles – levels of engagement

▸ Talk about the different levels of friendship. Notice the different things said to people at different levels and the different situations they share.

▸ Remind young people that they do not have to be friends with everyone at school but they do have to be polite – and ,hopefully, friendly.

▸ Close friends are very special and take time to make. It is not possible to be close friends with people we do not 'click' with but it is possible to be friendly to them, especially if they have not been mean or disrespectful.

- Everyone deserves to be treated with politeness and courtesy, even if they have been mean or disrespectful.

- Write in the names of people at each level of friendship.

Page 2: Friendship skills

- Discuss the ideas in the checklist – draw attention in particular to jealousy, forgiveness and self-control.

- Use the checklist to suggest ways of making friends.

- Monitor progress.

The game – Friendly Friends

Friendly Friends is a game about friendships designed for children between 5 and 12. Social dilemmas are presented for players to resolve. The concepts of friendship, friendliness, politeness and conflict are discussed. Include a child with good social skills in the game as a peer model. Game leaders model friendly skills and use problems that arise between players as teachable moments. Playing the game with children who exclude or are mean to others can be an effective way to encourage politeness, friendliness and kindness while outlining behaviour expectations. It is important that playing the game is not the only intervention used with socially isolated children or children who bully and socially exclude others.

Equipment

Board game, Little Friends, F-Cards, Questions, dice, tokens, prizes.

Aim

To collect as many Little Friends as you can while solving problems in friendly ways.

Before starting

Work out some basic rules – listening to each other, waiting for your turn, and saying nice things. Cover the main teaching points while explaining the game. Choose question cards suitable for the developmental stage of the players. Keep things balanced between talking and playing. Make up 'scripts' or short sayings from the following teaching points to use during the game:

▶ There is a difference between being friends with someone and being friendly and polite.

▶ We share special times and things with friends, such as hugs, secrets, toys, games.

▶ There are lots of friendly things we can do with people who are not our friends – share, help, play, co-operate, invite, join, be kind.

▶ We are polite to everyone at school, even if we don't like them – say 'thank you', 'please', 'excuse me'.

▶ It is friendly to invite others to play with us, especially if they don't have many friends.

▶ It's OK to get help if you are bullied – parents, carers, teachers, head teachers, friends, mediators, counsellors.

▶ It feels good when you finish first in a game but it doesn't matter if you don't – it's just a game.

▶ Just because you turned over an unfriendly card doesn't mean you are unfriendly – it's just a game.

How to play

Play in small groups of up to six children. Discuss the social dilemmas in the questions and the meanings of the F cards. Accept all attempts to answer the questions and expand answers by asking other players for ideas. Sprinkle liberally with verbal reinforcers, for example, 'Thank you for waiting' (sharing, using manners, telling us that). Respectfully help children resolve any problems that arise. Hand out small prizes at the end, for example, stickers, lollies, pipe-cleaners, plasticine, lucky dips, badges, pens etc. Smile lots and have fun.

F cards

▶ Choose a card and read it out. Talk about the meanings of the words.

▶ If it is friendly, collect a Little Friend.

▶ If it is not friendly, try again next time.

Questions

▶ Choose a question, read it out and suggest a solution.

▶ If the solution is friendly, collect a Little Friend.

▶ If the solution is not friendly, try again next time.

▶ If they cannot think of a friendly solution, ask other players for ideas.

Share-a-Friend

▶ A Little Friend token is shared with the person on the left by placing it between the two players.

Bossy Boots

▶ Return a Little Friend to the pack.

Rainbow highway

▶ If you land on the rainbow highway, choose a colour and read out the words.

▶ Go to the end of the rainbow and choose a Question or an F card.

Continue until all the friends are won – have fun!

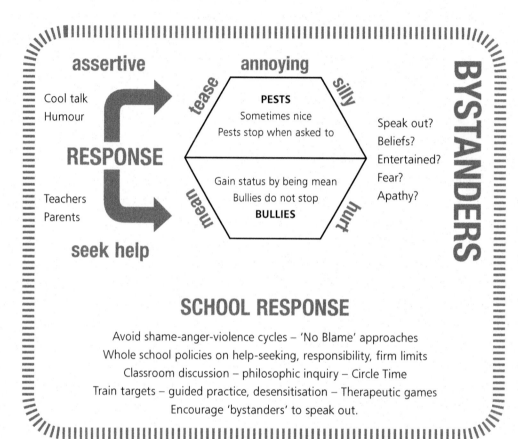

assertive   annoying

Cool talk
Humour

tease

PESTS
Sometimes nice
Pests stop when asked to

silly

RESPONSE

Gain status by being mean
Bullies do not stop
BULLIES

Teachers
Parents

mean   hurt

seek help

Speak out?
Beliefs?
Entertained?
Fear?
Apathy?

BYSTANDERS

SCHOOL RESPONSE

Avoid shame-anger-violence cycles – 'No Blame' approaches
Whole school policies on help-seeking, responsibility, firm limits
Classroom discussion – philosophic inquiry – Circle Time
Train targets – guided practice, desensitisation – Therapeutic games
Encourage 'bystanders' to speak out.

Chapter Seven

Resilience: Pests and Bullies

Sorting out teasing, bullying and fighting can be frustrating and overwhelming. The task is made urgent by the damage being done to vulnerable young people, sometimes for life. Being bullied puts one at higher risk of social difficulties, reduced academic performance, school refusal, physical illness, depression and suicide. Perpetrators too, are adversely affected long term by lower school attendance, criminal activity, depression and suicide. Bullying is a harmful interaction used variously to establish group identity, cohesion, excitement, status or to gain material goods. Young people who bully usually learn the strategies while watching the power struggles of other bullies, at home or school, adults or peers. The targets of this behaviour generally do not have the resources, skills or status to counteract the cycle that makes them even more vulnerable. Meanwhile the task is made difficult by those who stand by, adults or peers, through apathy, misunderstanding or lack of courage. Beliefs such as 'it will toughen them up' or 'you can't stop it anyway' freeze many into a state of inaction. Sometimes fights amongst children are labelled bullying when in fact all parties are 'giving as good as they get' and perpetuating the problem.

Reducing the incidence of teasing and bullying is a crucial step in increasing wellbeing and learning across the whole school community. Schools need clear policies and procedures that let students know they have a right to attend safe and friendly schools. Each incident should be challenged seriously and sensitively, with respect and understanding. Firm limits are needed around harmful behaviours, while avoiding shame – anger – violence cycles, in targets and perpetrators. Philosophic discussions are held in the classroom where issues of power, respect, fairness and caring are debated. Moral development helps young people develop the courage to speak out against injustice. Targets of teasing need the opportunity to develop a range of skills to make them resilient to teasing and seek help for bullying. Self-confidence increases through learning to be assertive, by having a repertoire of things to say and do, and knowing when to seek help. Playing 'Tease' desensitises the experience and provides a safe, fun environment in which to practice new skills.

It is important that working with the target is not the only response to teasing and bullying and that whole-school approaches are in place. Young people who tease and bully should be invited to take responsibility for their behaviour, to see things from the other person's point of view and to make suggestions about how to resolve the situation and restore the rights of the target to attend a safe school. No Blame approaches (Maines and Robinson, 1997), peer mediation and Circle Time discussion are examples of restorative practices that protect dignity and relationship while exploring bullying and teasing.

Pests, bullies and bystanders

Young people tease and bully for various reasons and characterising them as 'pests' or 'bullies' helps the target decide on a response. In simple terms, bullies victimise others by saying or doing unpleasant things and do not usually stop without close monitoring by adults. Immediate 'help-seeking' responses are required if children are the target of a bully. Pests on the other hand are silly and annoying kids who might just go along with a bully because they want to belong to the group, or to avoid being bullied themselves. Often they are polite and friendly when a bully is not around and will stop their behaviour when they think about the distress being caused. Pests can be met with assertive or humorous responses. Courage to be assertive builds positive self-concept and protects against shame. Knowing when to be assertive or funny and when to seek help is important when young people first start trying new behaviours.

Bystanders ignore what they see or say nothing through fear or apathy, or because they are entertained by it all. Philosophic discussion about character and who we are becoming can expand moral development and develop empathy through perspective taking.

Scripts, humour and cool talk

Words can help solve problems or they can make things worse. Positive, assertive scripts evoke a sense of calm control:

'I'll get help if you don't stop.'	versus	'I'll tell on you.'
'Call me by my name please.'		'You're the idiot, not me.'

Humour can defuse situations, especially where pests are involved. However, there is a fine line between being funny and being mean and the consequences of getting it wrong are quite serious, especially if a bully is involved. 'Non-committal' responses can also defuse situations and empower young people without the risk of offence:

| 'Mmmmm – very interesting.' | 'Well, well, well.' |
| 'I don't care.' | 'Wow – I never knew.' |

'Cool talk' is a formula for assertive communication. For example: When you call me an idiot it annoys me and I would like you to call me by my name. If you don't stop, I'll get help. This is simplified for younger children to Stop it or I'll get help. The formula is as follows:

When	(state the problem). . . . .
I feel.	(say how you feel) . . . .
And I would like.	(say what you want). . . . .
And if you don't.	(say what you will do) . . . .

Behaviour rehearsal

Children need to work out what assertiveness looks like and sounds like. Playing 'Tease' provides opportunities for guided practice in using cool talk and body language, seeking help, helpful thinking, self-calming, using humour and non-committal scripts. Playing with a bunch of well-adjusted peers provides a range of other coping strategies to explore. Offer guidance around deciding whether to be assertive or seek help when dealing with a pest or a bully. It may be a wise policy to always be polite when dealing with a bully. Identify which adults or peers the young person would approach for help.

Teachers, parents and carers

Teachers, parents and carers need to closely monitor children when they are first learning to be assertive. Potentially dangerous situations can develop where an escalation of bullying or verbal aggression and body posturing replace physical violence. Requests for help must be met immediately until the problem resolves. It is easy to feel frustrated by what is happening. Continue to support the young person and make sure policies and practices are followed to stop the bullying. Model confidence and optimism and use reflective listening to validate feelings and show understanding. Boost self-confidence by focusing on strengths and the things that are going well. Avoid exaggeration or victimisation of the target.

'Let's find a way to solve this problem.'	versus	'I'm sick of this.'
'You're a great kid just the way you are.'	versus	'Kids always pick on you.'
'Get help from the teacher.'	versus	'Tell on them – hit them.'

Young people who may benefit

Most students being teased and bullied will benefit from individual and small group training in social skills and assertiveness. The reflection sheets and game desensitise the experience of teasing while providing safe opportunities to practice responses to teasing and bullying in a fun, safe environment. In no way should skill development place the blame for harassment onto the target. It is not their fault nor is it their responsibility to make it stop.

Perpetrators who fit the characterisation of a pest might benefit from the opportunity provided in 'Tease' to see things from the other person's point of view. Likewise with the 'bully', only start one-to-one before slowly increasing the size of the group. Cease if they are unable to manage working with a group in friendly ways.

When to seek professional help

If the young person continues to show signs of anxiety or depression across a school term, such as not wanting to go to school, complaining of feeling sick in the morning, being tired all the time, clinging to adults, going over and over things, getting angry over little things, seek help from the school counsellor or educational psychologist. Early intervention is needed to prevent ongoing anxiety or the development of depression. Bullying behaviours will also need to be addressed. Firmer policies and professional help for perpetrators may be necessary.

Coaching sessions

In your introduction, explain how you will work together to learn some ways of dealing with teasing and bullying. Say something along the lines of…

'Often, when kids tease others, it's because they like to get that person upset. I'd like to talk with you about 'staying calm' and the kinds of things you might do and say to help. If you keep your cool, kids usually stop teasing after a while. I'd also like to talk to you about what to do if they won't stop after you ask them to.'

Use the reflection sheets to find helpful ways of thinking, to work out self-calming strategies and practice being assertive and seeking help. Read the story in the reflection sheets to give an overview of what you will be doing. Empathise with the young person's account of being teased and identify symptoms of anxiety. Explain how the body gives us early warning signs when we are getting upset and how we calm ourselves with relaxation, breathing and thinking straight. Explore the characteristics of pests and bullies and how we can respond in different ways to them. Look at the 'Pest' and 'Bully' plans and highlight anything that works for the young person and things they might like to try. Work out which adults they would ask for help if they needed it. Talk with these people later and explain how they might help the student. Fill in the questionnaire and work through any issues that arise.

Play 'Tease' together to reinforce the teaching points and role-play different scenarios. Invite a small group of others to play and explore the different ways they deal with teasing and bullying. Explore the consequences of the different ideas that come up, making sure players understand the difference between a pest and a bully, being assertive and being aggressive and being funny or being mean.

Talk to parents, carers and teachers about their progress and how they can encourage self-calming, assertiveness, helpful thoughts and help-seeking. Monitor progress over the weeks and celebrate successes. Check the teasing and bullying has ceased. Refer the young person and their family to educational services if significant symptoms remain after one or two months.

Pests and bullies – reflection sheets

The reflection sheets are in the form of a story. Read the story together and talk about the things that come up. Personalise the reflection sheets with colours, words and highlights and add the young person's own experiences to the story.

Page 1: This is an introductory page. Add things that the young person likes about school.

Page 2: Talk about the experience of being teased or bullied for the young person.

Page 3: 'Pests and bullies'

- ▶ Pests and bullies are different and are treated differently.

- ▶ Talk about the 'pests and bullies' in the young person's social environment.

- ▶ Introduce the idea of talking to parents and teachers.

Page 4: Helpful thinking

▸ Talk about the potentially damaging effects of allowing hurtful comments become part of how we see ourselves.

▸ Work out more helpful thoughts that are personal to the young person.

Page 5: Calm Plan

▸ Identify the young person's physiological reactions.

▸ Use them as an early warning sign to remind them to use their self-calming strategies.

▸ Work out a personal calm plan.

▸ Talk about courage and persistence.

▸ See Chapter Five, page 52 for instructions on 'tapping'.

Page 6: Pest Plan

▸ Talk about being assertive and how this is different from being aggressive.

▸ Explore the fine line between saying something funny and saying something nasty.

▸ Things may get worse if we are mean.

▸ Work out some assertive or cool things to say. Use the 'cool talk' formula:

Say: When. . . . . (say what happened)

I feel . . . . (say how you feel)

and I want . . . . (say what you want)

or I will . . . . (say what you will do).

This is simplified for younger children, for example, 'Stop it or I'll get help.'

Page 7: Bully Plan

▸ Talk about bullying behaviours and seeking adult help when dealing with bullies. Name at least one adult they could get help from at school.

▸ Identify safe places at school.

- ▶ Discuss the importance of politeness and what this means in relation to a bully.

- ▶ Talk about the importance of body language, standing and speaking confidently. Model how this looks and sounds. Have the young person practice standing tall and straight. Look at people when talking, head up, use a brave voice. Don't cry in front of a bully.

- ▶ Reinforce that it's OK to get help from adults.

Page 8: Practicing new skills and helpful people

- ▶ Talk about practicing new behaviours.

- ▶ Identify helpful people in the school.

Page 9: Questionnaire

- ▶ Use question 2 to assess how much the teasing/bulling experience is affecting them.

- ▶ Rehearse funny things to say to pests with question 5.

- ▶ Practice identifying pests and bullies with question 6.

- ▶ Encourage assertiveness and help-seeking.

The game – Tease

Tease must be played with a skilled game leader because players are asked to read out 'teases' to each other and there is a potential for things to be taken seriously. Hint cards suggest things to do and say, including humorous things to say when the teased. Explore the difference between pests and bullies, being assertive and being aggressive and being funny and being mean. Identify adults to approach when help is needed. Explore different things to say and do. Model self-calming strategies, humour and 'cool talk' during the game. Make observations and devise further interventions where necessary. Important: coaching targets of teasing and playing Tease does not replace the responsibility of the school for stopping teasing and for providing interventions for perpetrators.

Equipment

Board game, Tease Cards, Hint Cards, Money, tokens, dice, prizes.

Aim

Collect as much money as you can while collecting Hints for responding to the Teases.

Before starting

Work out some basic rules – listening, waiting, and saying nice things. If necessary, identify emotional first-aid strategies for anyone who gets upset while playing. Cover the main teaching points while explaining the game. Use Hint Cards to discuss different responses. Add teases that children have experienced to the Tease Card pack. Players must understand and agree to these two rules before starting:

Do not take offence to the teases that are read out.

Try not to hurt anyone's feelings when you read out the teases.

Main teaching points

Make up scripts or short sayings from the following teaching points to use during the game:

▶ It's just a game to practice what to do if we are teased – have fun and laugh.

▶ Everyone has the right to come to school without being teased or bullied.

▶ Someone saying you are 'stupid' or 'weak' or a 'red-nosed rabbit' doesn't make it true.

▶ When we say something back, being funny is OK – being mean will make things worse.

▶ 'Pests' and 'bullies' are different and we handle them in different ways.

- We stand up for ourselves when a 'pest' is annoying us.

- Bullies do not usually stop when you ask them – get help from adults to make them stop.

- It is OK to ask adults for help They are responsible for making teasing or bullying stop.

- There is a difference between standing up for ourselves and being aggressive.

- Be polite to everyone at school, including 'pests' and 'bullies'.

How to play

Play in groups of up to six children. Include emotionally resilient players as peer models. Start on GO with £100 and a Hint Card. Follow the directions on the board, including actions such as standing up straight and tall. Keep a balance between talking about the teaching points and playing the game. Sprinkle liberally with verbal reinforcers, for example, 'Thank you for waiting' (sharing, using manners, telling us that). Respectfully help resolve problems that arise. Hand out prizes at the end – stickers, pipe-cleaners, plasticine, lucky dips, badges, pens, dried apricots etc. Smile lots and have fun.

Tease squares

- Pick a Tease Card and pass it to the person on the right to read it out.

- Choose a Hint to respond to the tease. Receive £50 from the Tease reader.

- If a player does not have a Hint – think of an idea or buy a Hint for £50.

Hint squares

- Pick a Hint and read it out. Keep it until 'teased' in the game.

- Talk about the ideas and whether they would work for a pest or bully.

- When 'teased', choose the best Hint, read it out and return it to the pack.

Pests and bullies square

- Talk about the difference between a pest and a bully.

Stay calm square

- Talk about calming ideas – taking a deep breath, walking away, have a drink, thinking 'calm down'.

Stand confidently

▶ Stand up tall with head up, shoulders back and look at the other person.

Getting help

▶ Say who you would ask for help if you were being bullied.

Continue until you are out of time or money – have fun!

ANXIETY

INTERVENTION

- early intervention
- involve parents and teachers
- teach about physiology
- emotional first-aid plan
- problem-solving
- cognitive behavioural therapy
- identify support networks
- chart progress
- reward effort.

ADULT RESPONSE

- model confidence
- encourage facing fear
- matter of fact attitude
- avoid over-protection
- creative solutions
- have contingency plans
- be patient
- model emotional first-aid.

MOST COMMON PSYCHIATRIC DISORDER

- Cognitive signs – worries, nervous, inattentive, self-defeating
- Fears – strangers, dark, germs, insects, feathers, dogs, speaking
- Physical signs – stomach ache, headache, sweating, sore muscles, shaking, chest pain, dizziness diarrhoea
- Behaviour – clinging, inflexible, avoidant, distress, school refusal, crying, restlessness, aggression.

Chapter Eight

Anxiety: The Scariest Thing

Young people often express fears, worries and concerns as part of normal development which is an important part of maintaining safety and improving performance. However, anxiety disorders are amongst the most common psychiatric disorders affecting young people (about nine per cent) and when left untreated, can persist into adulthood (Kashini and Overschell, 1988). While the exact causes are unknown, inheritance, social environment and life experience have a role to play and effective intervention requires working with the families and teachers of such young people. The anxiety disorders are: separation anxiety, generalised anxiety disorder, panic disorder, post traumatic stress disorder, social phobia and selective mutism. Sometimes anxiety is not identified, even by parents, and is thought to be 'put on' or spoilt, attention seeking behaviour. Symptoms include:

▸ cognitive: irrational worries, nervousness, inattention, self-defeating thoughts, fearful

▸ fears – germs, insects, feathers, dogs, strangers, ghosts, etc

▸ physical – stomach-aches, headaches, sore muscles, sweating, over-breathing, shaking, chest pain, dizziness, diarrhoea, racing heart

▸ behaviours – clinging, inflexible, avoidant, distressed, school refusal, crying, restlessness, aggression.

Early intervention

With early identification and treatment, anxiety disorders can be effectively treated (Durham, 1993). Training in cognitive behavioural therapy (CBT) and self-calming prevents significant impairment (Mendlowitz et al., 1999; Silverman et al., 1999). One study showed that group treatment for six year olds over a period of eight to ten weeks produced substantial improvements which were maintained at a twelve month follow-up (Barrett et al., 1998). Successful interventions include the following approaches (Woolfenden, 2001):

▸ engagement of parents, carers and teachers

▸ teaching about the body's physiological responses to anxiety

▸ challenging negative thoughts and substituting helpful thoughts

- learning self-calming, relaxation techniques, for example, the slow breathing exercise

- using problem-solving strategies, taking positive action

- facing fears and becoming habituated to them

- identifying support networks

- charting progress

- rewarding effort.

Working with anxious young people

It is important for parents, carers and teachers to understand about anxiety and the therapeutic approaches being used and skills being taught so they can support and reinforce progress. If the coach is not in the school everyday, parents and/or teachers will need to monitor and chart progress daily for three or four weeks. Helping anxious young people sometimes creates a degree of anxiety or anger in the parents, teachers and coaches working with them. In your interactions, model confidence, patience, creativity and self-calming. Use reflective listening to validate the young person's feelings and provide reassurance. Gently and firmly encourage children to use their self-calming strategies while being brave and facing their fear. Normalise the routines and procedures of life with a 'matter of fact' attitude, as if 'everyone does this'. Parents dealing with school refusal might have to be creative in their response, for example:

- change arrangements for getting the child to school, for example, have dad drop them off if they cling more to mum

- use self-calming strategies yourself to deal with traumatic separations

- have a friend or teacher meet the child at the gate

- use discretion when deciding whether to pick up the child at recess or lunchtime

- avoid over-protection of the child

- make contingency plans for if things go wrong.

Young people who may benefit

These resources are designed for young people aged seven years old and up with mild to moderate symptoms of anxiety. Effectiveness depends on the child's cognitive skills and the experience of the coach. Students need basic language and thinking skills to catch unhelpful thoughts, challenge them and think of helpful alternatives (Kendall, 1994). If the young person is attending school, albeit with much persuasion, then their symptoms are probably not too severe to benefit from these approaches. These resources are also useful with students who have been involved in a serious incident and have lingering anxious feelings.

When to seek professional help

If the degree of distress remains the same or intensifies, or there is significant disruption to social and functioning and learning over a period of four or five weeks, then the family should seek specialist assessment and treatment from a educational psychologist or child psychiatrist. Treatment may include family therapy or medication. Sometimes graded exposure will be necessary and should be supervised by a educational psychologist or psychiatrist.

Coaching sessions

In your introduction explain how you will work together to learn some 'tricks' for beating scary thoughts and feelings. Say something along the lines of...

'I understand that sometimes things get a bit scary for you. I get scared sometimes too, most of us do. I'd like to show you some tricks and spells for beating scary feelings and getting on with the ordinary things other kids do, such as go to school, or walk upstairs, or walk past dogs or....... I've been talking to home and we would like to help trick the scary things.'

Parents and teachers are pivotal to the success of the intervention, especially over the first three or four weeks. Discuss the therapeutic intervention being planned and how they can help. Provide copies of relevant reflection sheets and invite parents to attend the first few sessions, if appropriate. Work out rewards with parents and teachers to acknowledge the young person's progress. Externalise anxiety by calling it something like 'the scary thing', depending on age, for example, 'even though the scary feelings were there, you were brave enough to use your tricks and spells and come to school anyway'.

Acknowledge how hard it must be to work up the courage to face the 'scary things'. Encourage the young person to commit to trying new ideas for the next three or four weeks. Tricks refer to positive coping strategies and spells refer to helpful things to say and think. Use the reflection sheets and game to explore anxieties, identify early warning signs, teach helpful ways of thinking, self-calming and problem-solving. Identify strengths and support networks. Teach relaxation, breath control and guided imagery techniques. Work out the 'tricks and spells' scary things use to trap kids and children's 'tricks and spells' to beat the scary feelings. Fill in the chart and talk about days when the bad feelings were smaller than others. Identify support people in the school and how they might help the student if they were feeling anxious.

Review progress over the weeks and celebrate successes. Play the game 'The Scariest Thing' with a small group of friends and explore how others manage their feelings. Normalise the experience of anxiety. Reinforce good role models. Discuss your exit from close involvement when appropriate and refer the family to educational services if significant symptoms remain over a month or two.

The scariest thing – reflection sheets

Share the reflection sheets with parents, carers and teachers to help generalise the strategies being taught. Modify the themes and scripts to match the age of the young person, for example, the theme of 'tricks and spells' might only appeal to a younger age group and use words such as 'strategies' and 'helpful thoughts' with older students. Use colour and words to personalise the reflection sheets.

Page 1: Identify the scary things on this page

- ▸ Have the student circle or colour the things identified as being scary.

- ▸ Explore the fear, noting 'faulty thinking', for example, a robber might shoot dad, or mum might get sick, or the germs will get me, etc.

- ▸ Talk about your own fears, if appropriate.

Page 2: Early warning signs

- ▸ Some people feel it in their tummies while others feel it in their heads, or neck or shoulders, etc. Refer to 'The Don't Get Eaten Machine' (Think Again sheet 4).

- ▸ Circle the parts of the body that the young person identifies as their physical response.

- ▸ Ask them to hold their hands apart to show how big the scary feeling is. This externalises the problem and shows that it changes over time.

- Use a ruler to measure how far apart their hands are and record this. If the young person cannot relate to this idea, use a simple 0 to 10 scale to rate the anxious feelings.

- Point out how early warning signs can remind us to follow our plan.

- Teach about relaxation and how it can make us and feel better.

- Practice physical release, guided imagery and slow breathing as relaxation techniques

Page 3: Helpful thoughts

- Introduce the idea of helpful and unhelpful thoughts. Read the thoughts and feelings and decide if they are helpful or not.

- Write negative thoughts or statements in the 'unhelpful' thought balloons – these are the spells the scary things use against us.

- Break the spells by changing them into helpful thoughts, for example, 'mum is a big person and if she gets sick she can ring the doctor – I don't have to be there.

- Helpful thoughts are our spells that help us beat the scary things.

- Challenge unhelpful thoughts by asking:

  'How likely is this to happen?' – 'Do I need help with this problem?'

  'Am I expecting the worst?' – 'Am I making things worst than they are?'

  'Am I expecting things to be perfect?' – 'Does it really matter?'

Page 4: Tricks and spells

- Tick those that apply and add any not listed.

- Watch out for these scary tricks and spells and use your own in return.

- If the student or their families are open to spiritual understandings, include prayer and belief as one of their strategies.

- Refer to chapter five for more ideas – Boss of the Worries, Floating Worries.

Page 5: Sample plan for someone who feels bad about coming to school.

- Talk about the ideas on the page.

- Write in some 'tricks and spells'.

- ▸ Identify friends and self-calming strategies.

- ▸ Catch unhelpful thoughts.

- ▸ Talk about the monitoring chart.

Page 6: Individual plan

- ▸ Build in ideas from the 'bag of tricks and spells'.

- ▸ Use gradual exposure to the fear provoking situation under advice from professionals.

Page 7: Progress and monitoring chart

- ▸ Draw the scary things – some students may prefer to draw the good things they will have if they beat the feelings – or use words.

- ▸ Tick every day the student beats the scary thing by overcoming their fear.

- ▸ Measure the size of their feelings with a ruler and record it on the chart.

- ▸ Discuss the issue of rewards.

Page 8: Problem-solving

- ▸ Step 1 Write out the problem. Explore the feelings around the problem. Ask about worries or fears. Work out what the student needs.

- ▸ Step 2 Brainstorm options without judging them – throw in some humorous ideas.

- ▸ Step 3 Evaluate each option by asking the questions and circle 'Yes' or 'No'.

- ▸ Step 4 Decide on a plan and who needs to know about it.

- ▸ Encourage the student to try their plan a few weeks and then evaluate it.

The game – The Scariest Thing

This game aims to develop resilience in young people with mild to moderate feelings of anxieties. The Tricks and Spells present a range of helpful thoughts and coping strategies. Helping others is encouraged throughout the game. Other kids love playing too and it is good to include positive role models when playing.

Equipment

Board game, Tricks and Spells, Bravery Awards, dice, tokens, prizes.

Aim

To get past all the scary things, help friends who are stuck and collect Bravery Awards.

Before starting

Work out some basic rule – listening to each other, waiting for your turn and saying pleasant things. Cover the main teaching points while explaining the game. Use Tricks and Spell cards to teach about self-calming strategies.

Main teaching points

Make up scripts or short sayings from the following teaching points to use during the game:

Physical things (Tricks)

▶ When scary things might happen, our bodies let us know, for example, sore tummy, headache, tight shoulders, short breath, fast heart, tight neck, chest, thoughts…

▶ When you feel scared, thank your body for telling you, take a deep breath and relax (shrug, stretch, tap a warning spot, remember your guided image).

▶ Slow your breath – equal in, equal out – to reduce feelings of panic. Counting steps as you walk is meditative.

▶ Drinking water helps us calm down.

▶ Decide what to do – acknowledge your feelings, relax, think straight, remember your plan, seek help if you need it.

Thinking things (Spells)

▶ Positive thoughts can make us feel better – negative thoughts make things worse.

▶ We can catch 'scary' thoughts and change them to 'helpful' thoughts.

▶ Positive thinking helps us be creative when we solve problems.

▶ Imagining a safe place helps us relax.

Doing things (Tricks)

▶ Make friendships, solve problems, seek help, think straight .

▶ Care for the body – eat good food, sleep well, exercise often, sit in the sunlight.

▶ Do your best, support each other, be fair.

How to play

Roll the dice and follow the path to the Bravery Awards, following directions along the way.

Tricks and spells

▶ Collect Tricks and Spells to get out of scary spaces.

▶ Read out the best Trick or Spell to solve a scary problem.

Scary spaces

▶ Players use tricks and spells to get out of scary spaces they are stuck on.

▶ If players have no Tricks or Spells, they wait for a friend or roll a six.

Go Help a Friend

▶ Go to where a player is stuck and suggest an idea to help them get out.

▶ Both players move to the edge of the scary space and wait for their next turn.

Speech space

▶ Just for fun, have players make a little speech if they land on the Speech space.

Bravery awards

- ▶ Players receive a handshake and a Bravery Award when they arrive at the end.

- ▶ Return to the Start to continue.

Continue until all Bravery Awards are won or time runs out. Good luck and have fun!

ANGER

JUSTIFIED
- Self-calming
- Problem-solving
- Seek help
- Restitution.

UNJUSTIFIED
- Self-calming
- Acceptance
- Helpful thinking
- Restitution.

early warning signs

school response

PHYSICAL

Fight – Flight
Increased heart rate
Tight fists, chest
shoulders
Sweating, headache.

COGNITIVE

Negative
Angry.

TIME
SPACE
THINK

RESTITUTION
CLASSROOM

Philosophic inquiry
Moral discussion
Teach – physiology
Social skills
Alternatives to
aggression.

EMOTIONAL FIRST-AID

Chapter Nine

Anger Management: Think Again

Most of us become angry at times but for some young people aggressive, angry outbursts are frequent events that isolate them from peers and adults in their social environment. Being able to control one's feelings and deal with frustration without resorting to aggression are fundamental skills to forming relationships with others. Interpersonal situations are the main trigger for anger: frustration, embarrassment, social rejection, conflicting goals, anxiety, worry, sadness, injustice, hurt, annoyance, grief (Riches, 1998). So in some ways anger can be viewed as a social act or construct, yet it is more complex than that. Genes, life experiences and the way we process information also influence the way we react. No simple solutions exist and only some of the solutions lie within the young person themselves. Early intervention programmes that are eco-systemic, that look at supporting families and schools are essential to breaking cycles of disadvantage. At the same time, young people can learn a set of behaviours that will help them navigate their social worlds. Through direct teaching, guided practice and modelling, children can learn self-regulation, interpersonal skills, alternatives to aggression, processing information, stress management, moral reasoning (Goldstein, 1988).

Physical responses and self-calming strategies

Young people can really benefit from knowing about the physiology behind their feelings. It provides a framework for gaining control and calming the self. The flight-fight response is protective and has developed over aeons of human evolutionary history. However it is usually inappropriate in our culture to react to perceived threats by running away or being aggressive, especially at school where children are expected to stay and resolve issues. The bodymind gives clear signs when threats are perceived and the neuropeptides are felt in the body as increased heart rate, rapid breathing, headache, sweating etc. (Pert, 1999). These physical sensations can be used as early warning signs for the need to calm down. The trick is to catch those moments between stimulus and response, sometimes only a few seconds, and to use well-known self-calming strategies. The relaxation response is created by a different set of neuropeptides (endorphins) which are triggered by guided imagery, slow breathing, helpful thinking, time out, drinking water, mindfulness and smiling.

Prosocial skills

Young people who lack the pro-social skills required to negotiate conflict and deal with frustration often have difficulty understanding and keeping social rules. They are quick to defend the self and faulty perception and interpretation of social interactions means they are more likely to ascribe aggressive intent to others. Peer difficulties arise and physical, academic and mental health problems reach across their lifetimes (Goldstein, 1988). According to Goldstein, teaching, modelling and rehearsing prosocial skills is an effective intervention into anger and aggression cycles. Training covers basic skills such as saying thank you, listening, joining groups, negotiating, coping with teasing, being a friend and co-operating. Advanced social skill training includes dealing with feelings, alternatives to aggression, dealing with stress, planning skills and moral development.

Justified anger

In some ways anger is protective and quite often justified, so knowing if it is or not is an important step in anger management. When anger is justified, young people need to calm their physiological response so they can engage assertively in the problem-solving process. They also need to decide at which point they would seek help to resolve the problem if they needed to. When anger is not justified, young people need to accept this and use self-calming strategies and helpful thoughts to help them move on.

Crisis points provide excellent opportunities for social, moral and cognitive development to occur through philosophic inquiry into the issues young people are facing. Explore the 'good' and 'not-so good' aspects of anger and invite them to take responsibility for making amends and avoiding further harmful reactions. Collapse time by looking ahead to the kinds of relationships they want throughout their future. Most would say they want respectful, trusting and loving relationships with others.

Young people who may benefit

Young people from aged six or seven years and up will benefit from learning about anger, depending on their thinking and learning skills. They need basic language skills, the ability to listen to others and to analyse their thoughts and body sensations. They need to be willing to talk about anger and try new ideas. Young people with serious chronic, antisocial behaviours might benefit, so long as coaching is only part of a multifaceted, eco-systemic programme.

Young people who do not respond over the course of a month or two will require specialist assessment for possible causes and treatments, for example, organic syndromes, psychological conditions, learning difficulties, child protection issues.

Coaching sessions

In your introduction explain how you will work together to learn some ways of dealing with anger and frustration. Say something along the lines of...

> 'We all feel angry sometimes and this is part of being human, but it is not OK to hurt anyone. We can catch anger early by listening to our bodies and stopping to remember our self-calming plan when we first feel angry. Then we can check out our thoughts and decide what to do to solve the problem.'

Use the reflection sheets to get an overview of the skills and strategies to be covered and to monitor progress. Identify issues of concern, strengths and gaps. Invite the young person to take responsibility for their anger. Talk about how much trouble it has been causing them. Encourage them to commit to trying new ways of thinking and acting for the next three or four weeks. Rate their current ability to manage anger and monitor this over the next few weeks. Work out their early warning signs and a personal emotional first-aid plan to help them calm down. Decide who else to share it with, for example, parents, teachers, friends. Acknowledge the challenges they are facing and how hard it is to manage at times. Look for 'exceptions' – times when they have managed anger well. Play 'Think Again' with a group of peers to reinforce the main teaching points and explore how other young people deal with feelings of anger.

Talk to parents, carers and teachers about how they can reinforce the skills being taught. Monitor progress and celebrate successes. If no further coaching is required, encourage teachers and parents to continue supporting the young person until healthy ways of managing anger are firmly in place

Reflection sheets – Think Again

Use the reflection sheets to teach about the body's physiological response to anger and to develop an emotional first-aid plan. Identify early warning signs and analyse potential challenges. Rehearse self-calming strategies and assertive communication. Use the rating scales to monitor progress.

Page 1: Optional introductory page

▸ Use words or pictures to represent themselves and anger, depending on their age. Older students will probably not want to draw.

Page 2: Who's the Boss – invitation to take responsibility

▸ Talk about how much trouble anger is creating.

▸ Ask about times when they have been boss of anger – what did they do to stay calm.

▸ Rate current control levels.

Page 3: Optional – Coaching

▸ Talk about how coaching works – negotiate how often and for how long you will meet.

▸ Share a little about yourself, especially any successful anger management stories.

▸ Discuss what might happen if the young person does not become the boss of anger.

▸ Gain a commitment to working on anger management together.

Page 4: Anger – the physiological response

▸ The 'don't get eaten machine' in our brains sends out 'neuropeptide' messengers to our bodies in response to threats or challenges.

▸ Our bodies get stronger because the 'neuropeptides' make us ready to fight or escape. This usually makes it harder to think straight.

▸ The 'don't get eaten machine' in our brains have developed over a long time and is a survival mechanism – such as the cave man running from the sabre tooth tiger.

▸ Even though we don't have sabre-toothed tigers in our modern world, sometimes our 'don't get eaten machines' still respond as if they are in danger.

Page 5: Early warning signs

▸ We feel the effects of the neuropeptides in our bodies, for example, stomachs, chest, neck, throats, shoulders, fists. These are our early warning signs.

▸ Identify where the young person feels anger in their body. If they have difficulty, use the 'Felt Sense' exercise to identify where they feel anger?

▸ Work out how long their fuse is, that is, the time they have between when they first feel their early warning signs and when they blow up and stop thinking straight.

▶ This is how long they have to remind themselves of their EFA plan. For some children this is a short time – they may need adults to remind them of their plan at those times.

Page 6: Emotional first-aid (EFA)

▶ Create time and space for self-calming to occur.

▶ Work out how long it takes to calm down and think straight after becoming angry.

▶ Rehearse responses to potential social dilemmas.

Page 7: EFA kit – tokens to manage anger and anxiety problems

▶ Work out the child's 'emotional first-aid kit'.

▶ Share the plan with parents, teachers, head teachers…

▶ Add ideas (blank token).

▶ Give a set number of tokens and gradually shape the behaviour by linking the tokens 'not spent' with favoured activities.

Page 8: Justified anger and cool talk

▶ Highlight any of the anger types the young person identifies.

▶ Practice cool talk.

▶ Rehearse self-calming strategies to deal with 'Unjustified Anger'.

Page 9: Challenges

▶ Use the 'What If..' cards from 'Think Again' to find challenges not listed.

▶ Focus on two or three challenges and explore problem-solving strategies.

▶ Discuss challenges that might require help from adults, for example, child protection issues, teasing, bullying, learning difficulties etc.

Page 10: Challenges and EFA

▶ Work out individual calming ideas and problem-solving strategies for each of the challenges identified.

Page 11: Monitoring progress

▶ Have the young person rate themselves against anger.

▶ Check progress with teachers, parents. Celebrate progress.

The game – Think Again

Think Again teaches young people about managing anger and thinking before they act. 'What If....' cards present social dilemmas to solve in calm, friendly ways. Calm cards present self-calming strategies, for example, talk sense to yourself, take time to calm down, have a drink of water, get help from adults, etc.. The difference between being assertive and being aggressive is explored. Tossing the Decision Cube (or spinner) introduces an element of chance that allows consequences for aggressive responses to be explored. Model respectful behaviour and teach scripts of calm and solution-focused language.

Equipment

Board game, What If.. Cards, Calm Cards, Spinner, Money, dice, tokens, prizes.

Aim

Collect money while using Calm cards to keep out of trouble and solve problems.

Before starting

Work out some basic rules – listening to each other, waiting for your turn, and saying nice things. If necessary, identify emotional first-aid strategies for anyone who gets upset while playing. Cover the main teaching points while explaining the game. Use Calm cards to teach about anger management strategies. Choose 'What If' cards suitable to the age of the players – add some of your own. Make up scripts or short sayings from the following teaching points to use during the game:

Physical things

▶ When we meet a challenge, our bodies let us know, for example, tight shoulders, fists, neck, chest, short breath, fast heart, sick, headache, angry thoughts...

▶ When you feel angry, thank your body for telling you, take a deep breath and relax (shrug, stretch, tap a warning spot, remember your guided image).

▶ Make your breath equal in and equal out. This helps balance the oxygen and carbon dioxide. Combine with counting steps to create a meditative response.

▶ Drinking water help us calm down.

▶ Decide if it is important or not – acknowledge your feelings, relax, think straight, remember your plan, ask for time out and seek help if you need it.

Thinking things

▶ Our thoughts influence our feelings and actions and sometimes make things worse.

▶ Catch 'angry' thoughts and change them to 'helpful' thoughts.

▶ Positive thinking allows us to be creative when we solve our problems.

▶ Guided imagery helps us relax – remember your calm place.

Doing things

▶ Make friends, solve problems, seek help, be strong, walk away if it is not important.

▶ Stand up for yourself when it is important – be assertive not aggressive.

▶ Care for your body – eat good food, sleep well, get lots of exercise and sunlight.

▶ Do your best, support each other, be fair.

▶ It's OK to ask for help when we need it.

How to play

Play in groups of up to five. Include a player with good social skills as a peer model. Players start with £100 and a Calm card and collect £50 for passing GO. Leaders read cards aloud if necessary.

What if...

- ▸ Read the What If... card aloud.
- ▸ Toss the decision cube (or spinner) and follow the directions.

Spinner or coin

- ▸ If the spinner lands on Think Again (or coin on Heads), think of a friendly way to solve the problem and collect £50.
- ▸ If it lands on 'kick fight bite hit swear threaten' (or coin on Tails), go to the Principal's office – unless you have a Calm card. Say how the Calm card might help you calm down and return it to the pack.

Calm cards

- ▸ Read the Calm card aloud and say whether this is a helpful skill for you.
- ▸ Keep the Calm card to get out of the Head teacher's office free.
- ▸ Return the Calm card to the pack after use.

Head teacher's (Principal's) Office

- ▸ Move to this square if the cube has sent you there unless you have a Calm card.
- ▸ Get out by rolling a 6 or paying £50.
- ▸ Visitors roll again.

Other squares

- ▸ Follow the directions on the board and talk about the issues raised.

CHARACTER VIRTUES

- Wisdom – perspective taking
- Courage – bravery, persistence,
- Love – kindness, generosity
- Justice – fairness, citizenship
- Temperance – self-control
- Transcendence – thinking of others, the environment.

C O P S

confidence **optimism** **persistent** **social skill**

ROBBERS

STEAL TIME AND ENERGY

TV / Video games

junk food

boredom

laziness

stress

anger.

Chapter Ten

Success at School: COPS

Success at school and life in general depends on a particular set of behaviours, attitudes and values. While excellent instruction, curriculum and resources are essential, it is the personal skills and habits that energise and motivate from within that create successful learners. Young people with these characteristics are resilient to the disadvantages life brings from home lives, learning difficulties, and unhealthy school climates. Fortunately research shows these skills can be taught and when taken on as a whole-school focus, students' achievement and social and emotional wellbeing increases (Bernard, 2000). According to Bernard, the four foundation keys are confidence, organisation, persistence and social skills and these are manifest in mind habits, for example, being independent, planning time, giving effort and playing by the rules.

With coaching, young people learn to set goals based on the things they value and work hard to overcome any hurdles along the way. They learn to check their thinking and to reward themselves for work done well. By practicing positive mind habits they can catch the 'robbers' that steal their time and effort. The resources in this chapter present these ideas in engaging and fun ways. Values are explored and opportunities for prosocial acts are presented in the game COPS and Robbers.

The COPS

The acronym COPS stands for the four foundation skills of successful students and the mind habits associated with them. With practice, these skills can beat the robbers, the things that keep us from achieving our goals. The four foundations are:

Confident

- self-acceptance
- independence
- 'I Can Do It' attitude
- look confident – body language
- think confident – positive 'self-talk'
- say positive things – the power of words

- learn from mistakes – this is how we grow
- have a go, take a chance, try something even though you're not sure.

Organised

- have goals, write down short and long term goals
- make plans, break tasks into bits, work out steps to take, prepare for Robbers
- write things down, make lists, tick off achievements, manage time, use a diary
- check instructions
- keep equipment organised – put things away, use containers and folders
- create a study space – have a working area, keep it tidy.

Persistent

- work hard, give effort – even when work is boring or hard
- keep trying – don't give up, remember Thomas Edison and the light bulb
- ignore distractions – especially noisy friends when you are working
- practice lots, develop skills, check your work.
- ask for help
- stay cool under pressure – manage stress and anger.

Social Skills

- develop self-control to handle difficult people and deal with peer pressure
- the Golden Rule – empathy – see things from the other person's point of view
- co-operate with others
- play by the rules
- Have fun with others – balance study and social life.

The Robbers

These are things that steal our time, take our energy and stop us from meeting our goals. They are time wasters and can be addictive. Identify Robbers and talk about how to beat them.

boredom	laziness	stress
tiredness	loneliness	hopelessness
teasing	unfairness	wasting time
resentment	some friends	forgetfulness
poor self-esteem	television	computer games
internet	junk food	drugs and alcohol

Values, virtues and character strengths

The things we do reflect our values and beliefs, which in their turn reflect our social cultures. Our character develops as we focus on the things we think are important; courage comes from facing adversity, wisdom from experience. We create personal and flexible hierarchies of values that represent our desirable or idealised ways of living. Values are the things we hold as important and Seligman (2003) says values based on the virtues of wisdom, courage, love, justice, temperance and self-transcendence lead to happy, meaningful lives. Materialistic and self-centred values are highly represented in popular media and young people too often find cultural heroes to emulate that reflect these values. This means it is important for us to be good heroes to our children, to find heroes among the stories in our literature and to hold philosophic discussions about beauty, love, values etc.. Remember, we all are works in progress and our character is forming with each new decision.

Goals and rewards

Talk about long term goals include life plans and career choices, for example, finish high school, go to university, save money to travel, join the team. Break long term goals into smaller steps to create short term goals. Encourage students to set goals from each of the four foundation keys. Create a reward menu in consultation with parents, carers and teachers, for example, extra time on a favoured activity – no trips to Disneyland! Talk about ways of rewarding ourselves, such as thinking, 'I did a good job on this project,' and giving ourselves simple treats. Aim for internal rewards and motivators such as satisfaction, gratitude and appreciation.

Young people who may benefit

These resources appeal to a wide range of young people, depending on their ability to wait and think about the dilemmas presented, usually from about seven or eight years of age and up. As a minimum, they need to be able to understand and use words to solve problems and be willing to work on concentration and impulse control. Be aware of learning difficulties, clumsiness and disorganisation. These children will need explicit, ongoing help with getting organised and keeping things together and some may need modifications and compensations in the classroom. The reflection sheets can be used with individuals, small groups or whole classes.

If these approaches have not produced noticeable gains after four to six weeks, further specialist assessment may be required to identify learning difficulties or other psychological factors. Refer students for specialist intervention if there are concerns around addiction to drugs or TV or the internet.

Coaching sessions

In your introduction explain how you will work together to learn some ways do be successful at school. Say something along the lines of...

> "COPS' is a game about being successful at school and in life. Successful students are (C) Confident, (O) Organised, (P) Persistent and (S) Socially skilled. They learn to watch out for 'time robbers' and work out ways to beat them...'

Use the reflection sheets to identify strengths and gaps and track progress. Encourage commitment to three weeks of 100% effort and explain that new habits take time to form. Make long and short term goals. Identify robbers and work out ways to beat them. Look at the values listed and highlight any the student thinks are important. Play COPS with the student and a small group of friends. Talk to parents, carers and teachers about the strategies being used. Review progress over the weeks. Celebrate successes. Discuss your exit from close involvement when appropriate.

Reflection sheets – COPS

Use the reflection sheets to explore the four foundation skills – confidence, organisation, persistence and social skills. Work out goals, robbers, rewards, goals, helpful thoughts, problems and values.

Page 1: Strengths, robbers and goals

- ▶ Highlight the skills the student already has.

- ▶ Tick the ones they wish to work towards – these become goals.

Page 2: Goals

- ▸ Choose a goal for the week and write it on the goal sheet.

- ▸ Think about what might stop them reaching this goal and what they could do about it.

- ▸ Who else (teacher, parents, friends) needs to know their plan so they can help.

- ▸ Write down some helpful things to say and think to help meet this goal.

- ▸ Work out a rewards.

Page 3: Helpful thoughts

- ▸ Talk about the connection between thoughts, feelings and actions, for example, if we think we are dumb, we will feel stupid and will try to avoid schoolwork.

- ▸ Introduce the idea of helpful and unhelpful thoughts. Read the thoughts and feelings in the box and decide if they are helpful or not.

- ▸ Catch negative thoughts and write them in the unhelpful thought balloons. Change them into helpful thoughts – 'I'm dumb' changes to 'I improve when I practice'.

- ▸ Challenge unhelpful thoughts by asking:

How likely is this to happen? – Am I expecting the worst?

Am I making things worse than they are?

Am I expecting things to be perfect or feeling not good enough?

Do I need help with this problem? – Does it really matter?

Page 4: Values

- ▸ Help clarify values by asking, 'Is this important to you'.

- ▸ Add values not listed.

- ▸ Sort values into 'Have now', 'Working towards' and 'Not important' groups – use the £ Cards from the game to do this.

Page 5: Problem-solving

- ▸ Step 1 Write out the problem. Explore the feelings around the problem. Ask about worries or fears. Work out what the student needs.

▸ Step 2 Brainstorm options without judging them – throw in some humorous ideas.

▸ Step 3 Evaluate each option by asking the questions and circle 'Yes' or 'No'.

▸ Step 4 Decide on a plan and who needs to know about it.

▸ Encourage the student to try their plan a few weeks and then evaluate it.

The game – COPS and Robbers

The aim is to catch Robbers using COPS Cards while collecting £ cards for helping stuck friends. Discuss the ideas on the COPS and £ Cards and talk about the 'Stick Around' things on the gameboard, TV, video games and junk food. The Cactus represents alcohol, cigarettes and drugs and discussion depends on the age of the players.

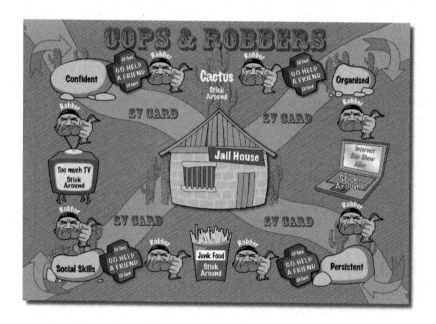

Equipment

Board game, COPS Cards, Robber Cards, £ Cards, dice, tokens, prizes.

Aim

Catch four Robbers with one of each COPS Card. Collect as many £ Cards as you can.

Before starting

Work out some basic rules – listening to each other, waiting for your turn, and saying nice things. Cover the main teaching points (above) while explaining the game. Keep things balanced between talking and playing.

How to play

Play with groups of about four students, depending on their age and ability to concentrate. Play in pairs if there are more than four players. Give one COPS Card to each player and talk about the idea on the card. Players start on the COPS Rock that matches their COPS card. Roll the dice, move in the direction of the arrows and proceed as follows when you land on these spaces:

COPS Rocks

▸ Pick a card (Confident, Organised, Persistent, Social Skill) and read it out.

▸ When you land on a COPS Rock, follow the path to Jail and release stuck players. Proceed in any direction on your next turn. Collect a £ Card.

Robbers

▸ Read out a Robber card and use one or your COPS cards to catch the Robber.

▸ If it does, place the Robber under the COPS Card on the table in front of you.

▸ If not, put the Robber back and go to Jail.

▸ If you don't have a COPS Card, go to Jail.

Stick Around

▸ Say if this is a problem for you and if so, say what you could do about it.

▸ Roll a 6 to be released or wait for another player to release you.

Go Help a Friend

▸ Go to a 'Stick Around' space or the 'Jail' and release players. Collect a £ Card.

▸ If no-one is stuck, stay on the Red Cross and collect a £ Card anyway.

Jail House

▸ Go to Jail if you cannot catch a Robber with one of your COPS cards.

▸ Roll a 6 to get out or wait for another player to release you.

£V Cards

▶ Collect a £V Card when you release players from Jail or Stick Around spaces.

▶ Say if it is important to you. If it is, keep it. If not, put it back.

Continue until someone catches four Robbers. See how many £ Values you collect. Have fun!

CAUSES

- genetic
- loss/pain
- disability
- reduced self-efficacy
- learned helplessness
- repressed anger
- distorted thinking
- metabolic processes
- cultural stereotypes.

SYMPTOMS

- suicidal
- poor mental function
- changed appetite/sleep
- loss of interest
- depressed mood
- physiological.

INTERVENTIONS

- psycho-education
- social support
- family therapy
- CBT
- medication
- stress management
- exercise
- relaxation/guided imagery
- philosophic inquiry.

CBT

Catch faulty thoughts

- exaggeration
- perfectionism
- jumping to conclusion
- ignoring facts
- catastrophising.

Substitute helpful thoughts

- realistic
- achievable
- positive
- based on facts.

Chapter Eleven

Coping: FishBowl

Challenges and stressors are part of life but for some young people, there are just too many at once and they feel overwhelmed, exposed and under scrutiny. Depression is a common response affecting between 5 to 12% of the population. Amongst the reasons for developing depression are genetic predisposition, loss, pain, disability, low sense of self-efficacy, learned helplessness, repressed anger, distorted or negative thinking and metabolic processes. With symptoms including depressed mood, loss of interest, changes in appetite, energy levels or sleeping patterns, hampered mental and physical function or suicidal thoughts or actions, it is essential to find ways of preventing and treating depression in young people. Effective non-medical approaches include education about depression, improving social supports, family therapy, cognitive therapy (changing distorted negative thinking), stress management, exercise, relaxation and guided imagery. Because of the potentially serious repercussions of depression and anxiety, it is important to seek specialist assessment and treatment when young people fail to make significant progress over a month or so. Sometimes medication is needed before they are able to use strategies such as cognitive behavioural therapy or relaxation.

Resilient kids have a range of coping skills and supports to protect them and many of these can be taught or put in place. School communities have a responsibility to set-up networks of mentors, counsellors, sporting activities, hobbies, clubs etc. to support young people. With the right attitudes and understandings, positive relationships create the sense of belonging that is so protective of children.

Cultural stereotypes

Cultural stereotypes of image perfection, strength, dominance, control, winning, materialism, and aggression are ubiquitous – movies, news programmes, reality shows, communities – and some young people will adopt these negative characteristics. They are particularly vulnerable when they fall short of their estimation of the ideal or if they are hurt or embarrassed by real or perceived attacks to their sense of self. Philosophic inquiry about these issues can help character development by discussing heroes that inspire young people to appreciate themselves and others and to live pleasurable, good and meaningful lives (Seligman, 2003).

Cognitive behavioural therapy

Unhelpful thoughts are often at the basis of depressed feelings. Cognitive behavioural therapy (CBT) is a proven effective strategy for working with children and young people who are feeling low or depressed. The strategies of cognitive restructuring are simple enough to learn but application can be difficult, especially when first being used. The trick is to be mindful of the fact we are having unhelpful thoughts in the first place. With practice, young people can catch thoughts, write them down, decide if they are helpful and if not, substitute helpful thoughts. Types of unhelpful thoughts include:

exaggerations.	'Everyone picks on me.'
jumping to conclusions.	'No wonder he doesn't like me.'
expecting perfection	'I can't do anything right.'
ignoring facts.	'I'm stupid.'
catastrophising.	'If I don't pass this exam I might as well give up.'

Take care not to use a series of platitudes or niceties when creating substitute, helpful thoughts. Make thoughts realistic and achievable, based on facts, and positive.

'Everyone picks on me'		'There are six girls in year nine who are unfriendly. I can get help from teachers and stay near my friends.'
'I'm stupid'	becomes	'When I studied for my last maths test I did pass it.'

Young people who may benefit

Children and young people with mild to moderate feelings of depression or anxiety can benefit from these approaches. Basic language, thinking and literacy skills are needed to hold a thought, write it down, evaluate it and think of alternatives. Even quite young children are able to understand the importance of helpful thinking and can learn how to catch their unhelpful thoughts. The reflection sheets are aimed at an upper primary level and above.

When to seek professional help

Young people with significant anxiety or depression symptoms need a team of professionals advising the family on case management issues such as medication, counselling and family interventions. Young people with suicidal ideations or talk of self-harm must receive help from a relevant professional as a matter of urgency. Parents, carers and teachers should examine their own thinking and model styles that do not exaggerate negativity or expect perfection. Some parents and teachers may need professional help to learn cognitive behavioural skills for themselves.

Coaching sessions

In your introduction explain how you will work together to learn some ways of dealing with feeling down. Say something along the lines of...

> '...sometimes the things that happen in life are so embarrassing we feel like everyone can see right through us, a bit like living in a fishbowl. The FishBowl game and reflection sheets teach about ways of coping that are not harmful. Over the next few weeks we can look at these ideas and have a bit of fun playing games with a group of your friends...'

Use the reflection sheets to identify issues of concern, coping skills, strengths and gaps and to monitor wellbeing. Acknowledge the difficulties they are facing and how hard it must be to cope with the pressures in their lives at the moment. Encourage them to commit to trying new ways of thinking for the next three or four weeks. Problem-solve tricky issues together and refer to chapter five for a range of coping strategies. Play FishBowl with a group of friends to explore which problems, skills and values other young people have. Reinforce any positive coping styles mentioned.

Talk to parents and teachers about how they can help develop positive ways of thinking. Review progress over the weeks and acknowledge any gains in positive thinking or mood. Discuss your exit from close involvement with the young person when appropriate.

Reflection sheets – FishBowl

Use the reflection sheets to assess the young person's social supports, mind habits, values and coping styles.

Page 1: Stress and resilience

▸ Look at the challenges and pressures coming from families, friends, school and themselves. Highlight any words in the fishbowl that apply. Add any that are missing.

▶ Talk about the words in the 'wall' of resilience. Identify the strengths they already have. Talk about times when these strategies have helped them cope.

▶ Choose ideas from the resilience wall to be the next goals.

Page 2: Helpful thoughts

▶ Teach about the connection between thoughts, feelings and actions, for example, if we think we are ugly, we will try to avoid people seeing us or interacting with us.

▶ Introduce the idea of helpful and unhelpful thoughts. Read the thoughts and feelings in the box and decide if they are helpful or not.

▶ Write negative thoughts or statements in the unhelpful thought balloons. Work out how to change them into helpful thoughts.

▶ Challenge unhelpful thoughts, for example:
Challenge worrisome thoughts. 'How likely is this to happen?'
Challenge fear and anxiety. 'Am I expecting the worst?'
Challenge exaggerations. 'Am I making things out to be worse?'
Challenge unrealistic expectations. 'Am I expecting things to be perfect?'
Challenge trivial matters. 'Does it really matter?'
Challenge their coping ability. 'What's the worst that could happen?'

Page 3: Values

▶ Highlight values that are important. Talk about why they are important.

▶ Add values not listed.

Page 4: Coping styles

▶ Use the rating scale on the right of each statement to show how often they use this coping strategy, ranging from 'not much' to 'very much'.

▶ Encourage positive coping styles.

▶ Talk about 'not so helpful' coping strategies. Help find alternatives.

Page 5: Problem-solving

▶ Step 1 – Write out the problem. Explore the feelings around the problem. Ask about worries or fears. Work out what the student needs.

▶ Step 2 – Brainstorm options without judging them – throw in some humorous ideas

▸ Step 3 – Evaluate each option by asking the questions and circle 'Yes' or 'No'.

▸ Step 4 – Decide on a plan and who needs to know about it.

▸ Encourage the student to try their plan a few weeks and then evaluate it.

The game – FishBowl

FishBowl simulates the embarrassing feeling of living in a fish bowl, open to examination by all. Playing FishBowl provides the opportunity for young people to explore the connection between thoughts, feelings and actions and to challenge unhelpful thoughts. The FishBowl cards present potentially embarrassing social situations. The FishFood cards present a range of ideas, skills and strategies that make young people resilient. The FeedBack cards allow players to give feedback on how they think someone else thinks about themselves and their ability to cope. It shows how well the young people know each other and gives feedback on how they are perceived by others. It is important when giving feedback that the player who is guessing is not making a judgement on the other person's coping skills, but having a guess at what answer the nominated person will give. A range of values and basic needs are embedded on the gameboard to allow exploration of what is important to young people.

Equipment

Boardgame, FishBowl, FishFood and FeedBack Cards, dice, tokens, prizes.

Aim

To give away as much FishFood as you can.

Before starting

Work out some basic rules – listening to each other, waiting for your turn, and saying nice things. Cover the main teaching points while explaining the game. Keep things balanced between talking and playing.

- ▶ Our thoughts influence our feelings and actions.

- ▶ We can learn to catch 'unhelpful' thoughts and substitute 'helpful' ones.

- ▶ Positive thinking allows us to be creative when we solve problems.

- ▶ We can use positive coping strategies that do not harm ourselves or others.

- ▶ We develop resilience by having friends, healthy living, helpful thinking, good work habits and values, positive family and community connections.

- ▶ Our wellbeing depends on a balanced approach to meeting our needs, including fun and freedom, as well as skill development and love.

- ▶ It is important to support each other.

How to play

Play with up to six players. Distribute FishFood to players and place leftovers in the central fish bowl. Start on a yellow box, roll the dice and proceed around the board following the arrows. Follow these instructions when you land on the following spaces:

FishBowl space

- ▶ Read out a FishBowl card. Tell how this situation would make you feel.

- ▶ Use the Think Straight balloons to create a helpful thought.

- ▶ If one of your FishFood cards helps the problem, put it in the central fish bowl.

- ▶ If not, other players may offer ideas from their FishFood cards. Choose the best one and place it in the central fish bowl.

FishFood space

- ▸ Pick a card from the central fish bowl and read it out.

- ▸ Say whether you think it is an important idea.

- ▸ Offer FishFood cards to other players when they land on FishBowl and don't have any cards of their own that help their problem.

FeedBack space

- ▸ Read out the person nominated at the top, for example, Person on your left.

- ▸ Read the card to that person and guess what answer they will give.

- ▸ Have the nominated person say if you were right or not.

- ▸ If not, how they would rate themselves?

- ▸ Give them some of your FishFood if it matches the issue.

Yellow squares

- ▸ Pick a word and comment on what it means to you and why it is important.

- ▸ If you have a similar FishFood card, place it in the central fish bowl.

Continue until someone gives away all their FishFood...or time runs out. Have fun!

PLEASANT LIFE   GOOD LIFE   MEANINGFUL LIFE

BEAUTY LOVE INTEREST SOCIAL SPIRIT

Authentic Happiness

Positive psychology – focus on positive emotions, virtues

Personal responsibility – make plans – delay gratification

Role of spirituality in mental health.

BlissBombs
challenges
selfishness
materialism
media bombardment
apathy.

Chapter Twelve

Authentic happiness: BLISS

Happiness is an eternal human pursuit sought across most cultures, even appearing in the constitutions of some countries as a basic human right. Aristotle, the ancient Greek philosopher said happiness is not a destination but a journey. Defining happiness is quite another matter, but at its simplest it is represented in positive emotions such as contentment, joy, ebullience and good cheer and it comes via many routes. There is mounting evidence that happiness, laughter and fun provide an antidote to stress and anxiety and all but the sadists would agree there should be more in our lives. Sounds easy enough, but too often the world crowds in and happiness seems elusive, so what it is and how we achieve it are important issues. Many live in disadvantaged circumstances, daily struggling to meet basic needs for food, clothing and shelter, or acceptance, let alone have fun or be free.

In the interests of making young people resilient to depression and anxiety, communities must intervene early into these 'disadvantage cycles' of poverty, ill health, problem housing and inadequate education. Lord Layard (2004), economics professor at the London School of Economics says the state can, and should, concentrate more on creating happiness in society through ensuring economic sufficiency and full employment to create a sense of optimism. Layard also suggests that as individuals, contributing to the happiness of others makes us happy in return.

Responsibility and materialism

Another feature of happiness is its link to personal responsibility or internal locus of control (Persaud, 2004). People who think they control their lives take personal responsibility for what happens. They make plans for the future and delay immediate gratification to reach long term goals. People with an external locus of control blame others for their problems and there is evidence of a cultural shift towards this in Western societies as evidenced by the culture of blame and litigation (Layard, 2004). Young people are subjected to media influences such as television, movies, music, games and heroes, all with messages to broadcast about what food, toy, image or action will make them happy. If materialistic, self-centred attitudes define values, then unhappiness is sure to follow with the disappointment of not having the exact right thing or look. A promising antidote to the unhappiness inherit in materialism is suggested in research into adolescent mental health. A recent review showed that greater levels of religious or spiritual practice lead to better mental health outcomes in adolescents (Wong et al., 2006)

Authentic happiness

From research into the emerging science of positive psychology (Linley and Joseph, 2003), it appears that optimistic thinking can be taught. Philosophic inquiry into happiness, virtues and personal strengths leads to better life outcomes for young people. Seligman's (2003) work in this area is bringing 'authentic' happiness into focus. Seligman describes the full life as:

> "....experiencing positive emotions about the past and future, savouring positive feelings from the pleasures, deriving abundant gratification from your signature strengths, and using these strengths in the service of something larger to obtain meaning." (Page 263)

Seligman writes of six virtues that are valued in many cultures and of 24 character strengths that reveal these virtues in our lives. Development of these virtues and characteristics leads to the enjoyment of a 'pleasant life', the gratification of a 'good life' and the purpose of a 'meaningful life'. With practice, young people can identify and build up their strengths and virtues to achieve a happy and fulfilling life.

- ▶ Wisdom – revealed through perspective taking, emotional intelligence, ingenuity, critical thinking, love of learning and curiosity.

- ▶ Courage – revealed through bravery, persistence and honesty.

- ▶ Love – revealed through kindness, generosity, loving and allowing oneself to be loved.

- ▶ Justice – revealed through citizenship, fairness and leadership.

- ▶ Temperance – revealed through self-control, caution and modesty.

- ▶ Transcendence – revealed through an appreciation of beauty, gratitude, hope, sense of purpose, forgiveness, humour and enthusiasm.

BLISS and the BlissBombs

BLISS is an acronym for Beauty, Love, Interest, Sociability and Spirit which represent the virtues and character strengths of authentically happy people. Appreciation of Beauty forms part of Seligman's 'pleasant life', Love, Interests and Social networks form part of the 'good life' and Spirit refers to the things that give us a 'meaningful life'. It is not possible, or desirable to remove all pressure from our lives, for it is in these furnaces that character is forged. The BLISS resources help coaches assess personal resilience and social supports.

Beauty

▶ The appreciation of beauty is a stress release technique – our brains release 'feel good' chemicals when we appreciate beauty.

▶ Discuss true beauty – nature, people, art, music, sport, dance, drama etc.

Love

▶ Belonging, loving and being loved.

▶ Appreciating love from family and friends.

▶ Giving, helping, sharing.

▶ Looking after ourselves – diet, sleep, exercise.

Interests

▶ Curiosity and enthusiasm.

▶ Hobbies and talents.

▶ Life long learning, finding out about things.

▶ Making plans, getting involved with projects, motivation, goal setting.

Social

▶ Reaching out to others, laughing (stress release), relaxing with friends, having fun.

▶ Co-operating, self-control, being polite and friendly, being a good citizen.

▶ Balancing everything all parts of our lives.

Spirit

▶ Developing a set of values – kindness, patience, gratitude, caring, forgiving.

▶ Striving for excellence.

▶ Having visions, hopes, goals.

▶ Becoming the true 'you', serving a higher cause.

BlissBombs

▶ Challenges to happiness – boredom, grudges, stress, schoolwork, feelings for example, tired, lonely, hopeless, scared, depressed inadequate.

Young people who may benefit

BLISS is for everyone. It provides a reminder of the important things in life. Young people who are sad or coping with challenges and adversity will benefit from the positive focus. With adjustment and simplification, these resources may be used with quite young children who will no doubt surprise you with their level of insight.

When to seek professional help

Refer young people for further assessment if they have not responded to intervention over the course of a month or two. Refer issues of self-harm, suicidal ideation, eating disorders, social withdrawal, body image distortions, unrealistic expectations, family crises, depressed mood or anxiety to relevant professionals like educational psychologists or child psychiatrist.

Coaching sessions

In your introduction explain how you will work together to learn some ways of being truly happy. Say something along the lines of…

'…'BLISS' is a game about being truly happy. Most happy people use the same sorts of skills and strengths to guard themselves against the downers of life. Research shows happy people appreciate beauty (B), love others and have love in their lives (L), are interested and enthusiastic about learning (I), are socially skilled and have fun with friends (S) have spiritual understandings, think about the earth and others (S). 'BlissBombs' are things that make us unhappy, if we are not careful'

Use the game and reflection sheets to teach about each of the different aspects of authentic happiness. Encourage young people to commit to three or four weeks of finding their strengths and values. Use the happiness scale to rate how happy they feel over the next few weeks and note that most people rate their happiness somewhere between four and six on the scale.

It is normal for feelings to go up and down. Play BLISS with a group of friends to explore strengths and values. Talk with parents and teachers about the skills being taught so they can use similar terms and be part of the celebration of progress. Review progress over the weeks. Discuss your exit from close involvement when appropriate.

Reflection sheets – BLISS

The reflection sheets provide an assessment of how resilient young people are. They can be used to set goals and map progress.

Page 1: Beauty

▶ Notice and appreciate beauty in all its forms – nature, art, mathematics, science.

▶ Teach about the physical effects of appreciating beauty on our brains and bodies and how this reduces stress levels – endorphins flood our bodies in response to beauty – the effect usually lasts for about 15 minutes.

▶ Beauty is in the eye of the beholder – discussion the true nature of beauty.

▶ Beauty is not limited to the way people look. True beauty comes from inside.

▶ Rate the young person's happiness on the scale.

▶ Identify the BlissBombs that an appreciation of beauty might resolve: too much to do, stressing out, nothing to do, hopelessness, feeling tired, sad, bored.

Page 2: Love

▶ Identify the groups of people the young person feels they belong to.

▶ Who do they feel love from? Do they appreciate this love?

▶ Who do they feel love for? How do they care for others?

▶ The Golden Rule says 'Love thy neighbour as thyself'. How does the young person care for themselves? Diet, sleep, exercise, doing nice things.

▶ Balance self nurturing and caring for others while avoiding selfishness.

▶ Identify the BlissBombs that an appreciation of love might resolve: parents won't let you go out, feeling down, unlovable, worthless, not good enough.

Page 3: Interests

▶ What do you like to learn about? What are you enthusiastic and curious about?

▶ What hobbies or talents are you working on?

▶ What projects are you involved with?

▶ What short and long term goals do you have? What would you like to study more?

▶ Identify the BlissBombs that developing interests might resolve: poor concentration, boredom, school work, hard work, tiredness, uninterested.

Page 4: Social

▶ Talk about good citizenship, teamwork, loyalty, self-control, playfulness, empathy humility, fairness, forgiveness, politeness, sharing, including others, cooperation.

▶ Identify the fun in the young person's life.

▶ Identify people in various friendship circles – friends, class mates, acquaintances.

▶ Talk about the balance between studying and relaxing with friends.

▶ Identify the BlissBombs that good social skills might resolve: holding grudges, loneliness, sad friends, meanness, anger, fighting, some people!

Page 5: Spirit

▶ Talk about creating 'a meaningful life' by serving something larger than ourselves, for example, caring for the environment, religious experiences, humanitarian service.

▶ Think about the character they are becoming – explore self-concept and ideals. What 'spirit' do they have, for example, a complaining spirit, a helpful spirit, a mean spirit.

▶ Discuss visions, hopes, goals, important issues – environmental, spiritual, humanitarian.

▶ Identify the BlissBombs that spiritual understandings might resolve: being mean, pollution, animals dying, helplessness, tiredness, unsure of whom you are becoming.

The game – BLISS

BLISS is a game about authentic happiness. The aim is to help young people develop healthy attitudes to life that will make them resilient to the ill effects of depression and anxiety. BLISS cards present character strengths that guard against the stress created by the BlissBombs. The healthy mind habits of happy people are explored. While playing the game, different types of happiness are explored: the immediate, short-term happiness of winning a game or seeing a beautiful sunset, and the long term happiness of reaching a goal or being respected and loved. NB: It is important that playing BLISS is not the only intervention for depressed or anxious young people.

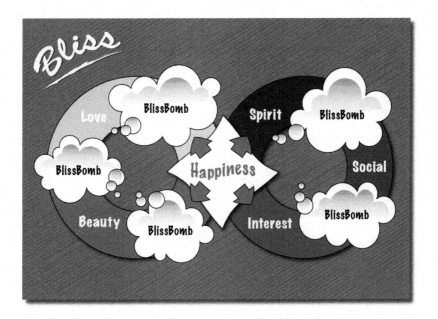

Equipment

Board game, BLISS Cards, BlissBombs, dice, tokens, prizes.

Aim

Catch five BlissBombs with one each of the five different BLISS cards.

Before starting

Work out some basic rules – listening to each other, waiting for your turn, and saying nice things. Cover the main teaching points (above) while explaining the game. Keep things balanced between talking and playing.

How to play

Play with groups of two to six young people. Start on Happiness, roll the dice and move in any direction.

BLISS: Beauty (red); Love (yellow); Interest (green); Social (blue); Spirit (purple)

> ▶ Pick a BLISS card, read it out and talk about what it means.

> ▶ Once you have a colour you cannot land on that space again. That means once   you collect a red Beauty card you do not land on the Beauty space again.

BlissBomb spaces

> ▶ Read the card out and decide if one of your BLISS cards meets the challenge.

> ▶ If so, place the BlissBomb on the table and cover it with the BLISS card.

> ▶ If not, put the BlissBomb back.

Happiness space

> ▶ Talk about what makes you happy and roll again.

> ▶ Players may change direction when they land on the Happiness space.

Continue until everyone has five BlissBombs covered by a BLISS Card.

Have fun!

References

Bandura, A. (1986) *Social Foundations of Thought and Action: A Social Cognitive Theory*. Englewood Cliffs, NJ: Prentice-Hall.

Barrett, P., Dadds, M. and Rapee, R. (1996) *'Family treatment of childhood anxiety: a controlled trial'*, *Journal of Consulting and Educational Psychology* 62(2): 333-342.

Barrett, P., Lowry-Webster, H. and Holmes, D. (1998) FRIENDS Program, http://www.australianacademicpress.com.au/friends/anxietydepress.htm (accessed 14 February 2006).

Bennett, H, and Disbrow, E. (1999) *Mind Body Medicine: How to Use Your Mind for Better Health*. Yonkers, New York: Consumer Report Books.

Benson, P. L., Leffert, N., Scales, P. C. and Blyth, D. (1998) *'Beyond the "village" rhetoric: creating healthy communities for children and youth'*, *Applied Developmental Science* 2 (1): 138-159.

Bernard, M. (2000) www.youcandoiteducation.com (accessed 3 March 2006)

Blum, R. (2000) *Healthy Youth development: A Resiliency Paradigm for Adolescent Health Development*, 3rd pacific Rim Conference of the International Association for Adolescent Health: Lincoln University, Christchurch, June.

Bower, B. (1998) *'Incriminating developments: scientists want to reform the study of how kids go wrong'*. *Science News*, 5 September, 153-155.

Butler, K. (1997) *The Anatomy of Resilience. Family Therapy Networks*, March/April, 22-31.

Coie, J. D., and Koepple, G. K. (1990) *'Adapting intervention to the problems of aggressive and disruptive rejected children'*, in S. R. Asher and J. D. Coie (eds), *Peer Rejection in Childhood* (pp. 309-337). New York: Cambridge University Press.

Conduct Problems Prevention Research Group (2002) *'The implementation of the Fast Track program: An example of large-scale prevention science efficacy trial'*, *Journal of Abnormal Child Psychology*, 30, 1-18.

Connolly, J. A., Doyle, A. B. and Reznick, E. (1988) *'Social pretend play and social interactions in preschoolers'*, *Journal of Applied Developmental Psychology*, (9) 301-313.

Cooper, P., Smith, C., Upton, G. (1994) *Emotional and Behavioural Difficulties* London: Routledge.

Davidson, W. S. and Redner, R. (1998) *'The prevention of juvenile delinquency: diversion from the juvenile justice system'*, in R. H. Price, E.

L. Cowen, R. P. Lorion and J. Ramos-McKay (eds), *Fourteen Ounces of Prevention: Theory, Research and Prevention (pp.* 123-137). New York: Pergamon.

DuBois, D. L., Holloway, B. E., Valentine, J. C. and Cooper, H. (2002) *'Effectiveness of mentoring programs for youth: a meta-analytic review'. American Journal of Community Psychology*, 30: 157-197

Durant, M. (1995) *Creative Strategies for School Problems: Solutions of Psychologists and Teachers.* W. W. Norton, New York.

Durham, R.C. and Allen, T. (1993) *'Psychological treatment of generalised anxiety disorder: a review of the educational significance of results in outcome studies since 1980', British Journal of Psychiatry*, 163: 19-26.

Fast Track Project, http://www.fasttrackproject.org (accessed 5 March 2006).

Fitzsimons-Lovett, A. (2001) *Things I Learned the Hard Way: Behaviour Management for Students with Aggressive and Violent Behaviors in Alternative Settings,* Latin-American Youth Center, Washington DC.

Fredrickson, B. L. and Joiner, T. (2002) *'Positive emotions trigger upward spirals toward emotional well-being', Psychological Science*, 13: 172-175.

Gerhardt, S. (2004) *Why Love Matters: How Affection Shapes a Baby's Brain.* New York: Bruner Routledge.

Gladwell, M. (1997) *'Damaged: why do some people turn into violent criminals?' The New Yorker*, 24 February: 132-138.

Goldstein, A. P. (1988) *The Prepare Curriculum: Teaching Prosocial Competencies.* Champaign, IL: Research Press.

Goldstein, A. P., Glick, B. and Gibbs, J. C. (1998) *Aggression Replacement Training: A Comprehensive Intervention for Aggressive Youth.* Revised Edition. Champaign, IL: Research Press.

Goleman, D. (1995) *Emotional Intelligence: Why it Can Matter More Than IQ.* London: Bloomsbury.

Gowen, J. and Nebrig, J. (2002) *Enhancing Early Emotional Development.* London: Paul H. Brookes Pub Co.

Greene, R. (2001) *The Explosive Child*. Second Edition. New York: Harper Collins.

Grossman, J.P. and Tierney, J.P. (1998) *'Does mentoring work? An impact study of the big brothers/big sisters program'*, Evaluation Review, 22: 403-426.

Halberstadt, A. G., Denham, S. A. and Dunsmore, J. C. (2001) *'Affective social competence'*, Social Development, 10: 79-119.

Hawley, D. R. and DeHaan, L. (1996) *'Toward a definition of family resilience: Integrating life- span and family perspectives'*, Family Processes, 35 (3): 283-298.

Hromek, R. P. (2004) *Planting the Peace Virus: Early Intervention to Prevent Violence in Schools*. Bristol: Lucky Duck Publishing.

Hromek, R. P. (2005) *Game Time*. London: Paul Chapman Publishing.

Jordan, J. (1997) *'A Narrative Account of a Teacher Researching and Changing Her Classroom Practice'*, Teaching and Teachers' Work, 5 (2): 1-9.

Kagan, J. (1998) *Galen's Prophecy*. Boulder, CO: Westview Press.

Karoly, L. A., Greenwood, P. W., Everingham, S. S., Hoube, J., Kilburn, S. R., Rydell, C. P. and Chiesa, J. (1998) *Investing in Our Children: What we Know and Don't Know about the Costs and Benefits of Early Interventions*, Santa Monica, CA: RAND.

Kashini, J.H. and Overschell, H. (1988) *'Anxiety disorders in mid-adolescence: A community sample'*, American Journal of Psychiatry, 145: 960-964.

Keltner, D. and Haidt, J. (2001) *'Social functions of emotions'*, in T.J. Mayne and G. A. Bonanno (eds), *Emotions: Current Issues and Future Directions. Emotions and Social Behaviour (pp.* 192-213). New York: Guildford.

Kendall, P. (1994) *'Treating Anxiety Disorders in Children: Results of a Randomised Educational Trial'*, Journal of Consulting and Educational Psychology, 62 (1): 100-110.

Kohn, A. (1993) *Punished by Rewards: The Trouble with Gold Stars, Incentive Plans, A's, Praise, and Other Bribes*. Boston: Houghton Mifflin

Kohn, A. (1997) *'How Not to Teach Values'*. Phi Delta Kappan, February, 429-439

Ladd, G. W. and Asher, S. R. (1985) *'Social skill training and children's peer relations'*, in L. L'Abate and M. A. Milan (eds), *Handbook of Social Skills Training and Research* (pp. 219-244). New York: Wiley.

Layard, Lord R. (2004) *Happiness: Lessons from a New Science. London:* The Penguin Press.

Linley, A. and Joseph, S. (2004) *Positive Psychology in Practice,* Hoboken, NJ: Wiley.

Lopes, P. N., Brackett, M. A., Nezlek, J. b., Schutz, A., Sellin, I. and Salovey, P. (2004) *'Emotional intelligence and social interaction', Personality and Social Psychology Bulletin,* 30, 1018-1034

Luthar, S.S. (2005) *'Resilience at an early age and its impact on child psychosocial development',* in R.E. Tremblay, R.G. Barr, and R. Peters (eds), Encyclopedia on Early Child Development [online]. Montreal, Quebec: Centre of Excellence for Early Childhood Development; 2005: 1-6. Available at: http://www.excellence-earlychildhood.ca/documents/LutharANGxp.pdf. Accessed 4 March, 2006.

Maines, B. and Robinson, G. (1997) *Crying For Help: The No Blame Approach to Bullying.* Bristol: Lucky Duck Publishing.

McCold, P. (2002) *Evaluation of a Restorative Milieu:* CSF Buxmont School/ Day Treatment programs 1999–2001 evaluation outcome technical report. Paper presented at the American Society of Criminology Annual Meeting, Chicago, Illinois. Available at: http://www.realjustice.org/library/erm.html Accessed 14 February 2006.

McGrath, H. and Noble, T. (2003) *Bounce Back! A Classroom Resiliency Program.* Pearson Education Australia, Melbourne.

McGregor, S. (1992) *Piece of Mind.* CALM Pty Ltd: Australia.

McPartland, J. M., and Nettles, S. M. (1991) *'Using community adults as advocates or mentors for at-risk middle school students: a two-year evaluation of project RAISE', American Journal of Education* 99: 568-586.

Miller, J., Fletcher, K. and Kabat-Zinn, J. (1995) *'Three-year follow-up and educational implications of a mindfulness-based stress reduction intervention in the treatment of anxiety disorders', General Hospital Psychiatry,* 17: 192-200.

Mendlowitz, S.L., Manassis, K., Bradley, S., Scapillato, D., Miezitis, S. and Shaw, B. F. (1999) *'Cognitive-behavioural group treatments in childhood anxiety disorders: the role of parental involvement', Journal of the American Academy of Child and Adolescent Psychiatry,* 38 (10): 1223-1229.

Montgomery, B. and Evans, L. (1984) *You and Stress.* Ringwood: Viking O'Neil.

Nathanson, D.L. (2003) *The Name of the Game is Shame*. Report to the Academic Advisory Council of the National Campaign Against Youth Violence http://www.tomkins.org/PDF/library/articles/thenameofthegameisshame.pdf Accessed17 March 2006.

Nucci, L. (1987) *'Synthesis of research on moral development'*, *Educational Leadership* February, 86-92.

Nucci, L. (1997) 'Moral development and character formation', in H. J. Walberg and G. D. Haertel (eds), *Psychology and Educational Practice* (pp.127-157). Berkeley: MacCarchan.

O'Connell, T. and McCold, P. (2004) *'Beyond the journey,* not much else matters: avoiding the expert model with explicit restorative practice', paper presented at New Frontiers in Restorative Justice: Advancing Theory and Practice, Centre for Justice and Peace Development, Massey University at Albany, New Zealand, 2-5 December.

Oden, S. and Asher, S. R. (1977) *'Coaching children in social skills for friendship making', Child Development*, 48: 495-506.

Persaud, R. (2004) *The Motivated Mind. St. Albans,* Bantam Press.

Pert, C. B. (1999) *Molecules of Emotion: The science behind mind-body medicine.* New York: Simon and Schuster.

Redl, F. (1966) *When We Deal With Children*. New York, The Free Press.

Reid, J. (1993) *'Prevention of conduct disorder before and after school entry: Relating interventions to developmental findings', Development and Psychopathology*, 5 (1/2): 243-262.

Reisner, E., Petry, C. A. and Armitage, M. (1998) 'A review of programs involving college students as tutors or mentors in grades K-12'. Washington, DC: Policy Studies Associates, Inc.

Rhodes, J. E. (2002) *Stand By Me. The Risks and Rewards of Mentoring Today's Youth.* Cambridge, MA.: Harvard University Press.

Richardson, A. (2004) quoted in 'A rotten way to feed the children', *Times Educational Supplement'* 16 April http://www.fabresearch.org (accessed 1 March, 2006).

Riches, V. C. (2004) *'Guns or roses: anger in the social context',* paperdelivered at NSW Department of Education and Training Special Education Conference, Sydney, Australia.

Rigby, K. (2002) 'A meta-evaluation of methods and approaches to reducing bullying in pre-schools and early primary school in Australia'. National Crime Preventions Programme. Canberra: Commonwealth Attorney General's Department.

Roffey, S. (2006) *Circle Time for Emotional Literacy.* London: Sage Publications.

Rutter, M., and Giller, H. (1983) *Juvenile Delinquency: Trends and Perspectives.* New York: Guilford Press.

Segal, Z.V., Williams, J.M.G. and Teasdale, J.D. (2002) *Mindfulness-based Cognitive Therapy for Depression: A New Approach to Preventing Relapse.* Guilford Publications, New York.

Seligman, M.E.P. (2003) *Authentic Happiness: Using the New Positive Psychology to Realize Your Potential for Lasting Fulfillment,* Sydney: Random House Australia.

Selman, R. (1981) 'The child as a friendship philosopher', in S. R. Ashman and J. M. Gottman (eds) *The Development of Children's Friendships* (pp242-272). Cambridge: Cambridge University Press.

Silverman, W.K., Kurtines, W.M., et al (1999). 'Treating anxiety disorders in children with group cognitive-behavioural therapy: a randomised educational trial', *Journal of Consulting and Educational Psychology,* 67(6): 995-1003.

Stoolmiller, M., Eddy, M. and Reid, J. D. (2000) 'Detecting and Describing Preventive Intervention Effects in a Universal School-Based Randomized Trial Targeting Delinquent and Violent behaviour', *Journal of Consulting and Educational Psychology,* April, 296-306.

Thomas, J. (1991) 'You're the greatest', *Principal,* 71: 32-33.

Tomkins, S. (1991) *Affect, Imagery, Consciousness Vol III: The negative Affects: Anger and Fear.* New York: Springer Publishing Co.

Tremblay, R. E. (2004) 'Development of physical aggression during infancy', *Infant Mental Health Journal,* 25(5): 399-407.

Villani, S. (2001) 'Impact of Media on Children and Adolescents: A 10-Year Review of the Research', *Journal of the American Academy of Child and Adolescent Psychiatry,* 40:392-401.

Vygotsky, L.S. (1962) *Thought and Language,* Cambridge, MA: MIT Press.

Vygotsky, L. S. (1976) 'Play and its role in the mental development of the child', in J. S. Bruner, A. Jolly and K. Sylvia (eds), *Play: Its Role in Development and Evolution,* 537-554. New York: Basic Books.

Vygotsky, L. S. (1986) *Thought and Language.* Cambridge, MA: MIT Press.

Walker, H.M., Colvin, G. and Ramsey, E. (1995) *Antisocial Behaviour in Schools: Strategies and Best Practices.* Pacific Grove: CA, Brooks/Cole.

Walker, H.M., Horner, R.H., Sugai, G., Bullis, M., Sprague, J.R., Bricker, D. and Kaufman, M.J. (1996) 'Integrated approaches to preventing antisocial behaviour patterns among school aged children', *Journal of Emotional and Behaviour Disorders,* 4 (4): 194-211.

Walsh, F. (1996) 'The concept of family resilience: Crisis and Challenge', *Family Processes,* 35(3): 261-281.

Wells, S., Polglase, K., Andrews, H.B., Carrington, P. and Baker, H.A. (2003) 'Evaluation of a meridian-based intervention, Emotional Freedom Techniques (EFT), for reducing specific phobias of small animals', *Journal of Educational Psychology,* 59 (9): 943-966.

Werbach, M. R. and Moss, J. (1999) *Textbook of Nutritional Medicine.* Third Line Press, USA.

Werner, E. E., and Smith, R. S. (1982) *Vulnerable but Invincible: A Longitudinal Study of Resilient Children and Youth.* New York: McGraw-Hill.

Wong, Y.J., Rew, L.and Slaikeu, K. D (2006) 'A systematic review of recent research on adolescent religiosity/spirituality and mental h ealth'. *Issues in Mental Health Nursing,* 27 (2) February/March, 161-183.

Wood, M. and Long, N. (1991) *Life Space Intervention.* Austen, TX: PEO-ED.

Woolfenden, S. (2001) 'Evidence based practice: what is the evidence that CBT works in childhood', *The Clinician: Child and Adolescent Mental Health Statewide Network,* 1(1&2): 38-40.

Zins, J.E., Weissberg, R.P., Wang, M.C.and Walberg, H.J. (eds) (2004) *Building Academic Success on Social and Emotional Learning: What Does the Research Say? New York:* Teachers College Press.